Faith on a Sticky Note

Mark McKinney

REDEMPTION PRESS

Published by Redemption Press,
PO Box 427, Enumclaw, WA 98022
Toll Free (844) 2REDEEM (273-3336)

Redemption Press is honored to present this title in partnership with the author. The views expressed or implied in this work are those of the author. Redemption Press provides our imprint seal representing design excellence, creative content, and high quality production.

ISBN 13: 978-1-68314-539-4

This book is dedicated to Betty C
McKinney – my mama, my friend.

Contents

Foreword

When I started reading *Faith on a Sticky Note*, I thought, "Here is another book on how losing a loved one turned someone's life around, and how after dealing with the guilt and anger over missing so many opportunities to tell the deceased how much he was loved, he realizes that Jesus is the hope for peace and salvation and a second chance to tell that loved one everything he wanted to say." I was right. Well, at least partially. What I realized as I read Mark's book was that I was reading words generated by someone who struggled and still struggles with his faith. Losing a loved one was merely the seed from which a great oak of faith has emerged. Mark not only got to tell his father everything he wanted to, he got to see his father saved. That is what makes this book different from any other inspirational book I have read. Even though intellectually Mark knew and knows his father is in heaven, he did not viscerally feel it. The book explains how the greatest faith springs from doubt. Mark also shares with the reader a modern perspective of Christianity and how to lead a modern Christian life that will resonate with the reader for a long time. I have not heard a sermon, nor have I read a book that so clearly outlines what we can do as Christians to strengthen our relationship with Christ while living in today's world. This is not a 'feel-good-about-yourself-because-you-can-do-anything-as-long-as-you-are-saved' kind of book. This book is an honest and genuine account of how today's Christian can be just that - a Christian - imperfect, sinful, human - and still develop a relationship with Christ."

Randy Smith, personal friend and fellow member of
Lincolnton Baptist Church

Introduction

I am sitting in church thinking, *"You are broken. Something is wrong with your inner workings if everyone sitting around you has had the "event" and seen the light, felt the shuddering, been overcome with joy, peace, or heard a voice..."* This inner dialogue *(talking to myself)* is all about the moment "it" happens ... being saved. Asking Christ to come into your life to lead you. My dilemma? I never saw, felt, or heard any of that stuff people talk about, even though I had asked Christ into my life. I had heard testimonies about it in Bible studies and sermons and got the idea that you should 'feel' the event, that you will know when it happens, and recognize it as a defining moment in your life – a true Damascus road experience. So, I immediately thought, *"I must not be saved, and I am sitting here amongst a bunch of haves, when I am a have-not. Surely, I cannot speak up and say anything lest I be judged for not being on the team, or worse yet, unworthy of being saved."*

I struggled with that for quite some time in my recent years – afraid to ask in fear of being exposed. Always nodding and saying, "Oh, yeeeeaah," when someone asked if I were saved, even though I did not have the ticket stub, so to speak, in the way of a story to tell about my moment of salvation.

I soon came to realize, though, with unquestionable clarity, that I am on the team, and that I am not the lone ranger when it comes to questioning one's own salvation.

This epiphany came about through a series of events and circumstances that I share in this book. It is one man's testimony, mine, paved with pieces of God's puzzle, including an alcoholic father, a career in sales, defining what "one in twenty" and "DNR" really mean, learning when to draw to an inside straight, Ronnie Milsap, banjos and a stand-up bass, flight attendant call bells, recruiters, freaks and weirdos, red corvettes, and a legendary football coach. My purpose in writing this book is to put forth what I have learned from all of the above and the theme that ties them all together, which I believe will resonate with you long after you turn the last page. My goal is to have an impact on your faith and your Christian walk. Even more so, it is to share with you my "Sticky note of faith" - what I believe is the single most important piece of paper that you can reference each day of your spiritual walk.

I am not a pastor, preacher, or reverend and have never been to the seminary. I am an individual living life just like you. In my everyday life, I am a software salesman traveling about 30,000 air-miles a year (*rookie stuff to you million-milers out there – my hat's off to you*) and getting the opportunity to meet many people and see many great places. I am the husband of one, father of two, and blessed to be a friend of many.

In addition to being a quota-carrying salesman, I am someone who is excited about what I have come to understand about Christ and my salvation. I feel strongly that this message can have a positive impact on anyone who is concerned about his salvation and can provide the clarity which I have come to appreciate. This book will not teach you how to interpret carbon dating samples, how to be a better singer of hymns, or even the difference between Methodists and Baptists; what it will do is provide you with a foundation to understand your faith, to embrace that faith, and to utilize it to impact every single aspect of your life and the lives around you, period.

My prayer is that this true story - this testimony - will impact you as much as it has impacted me in living it. I have cried, laughed, and learned countless things in this process, and if even one person starts or strengthens a relationship with Christ as a result of this effort, it is all worth it.

God bless and enjoy!

Mark McKinney

Chapter 1

CLEARED FOR TAKEOFF

"Lord, I thank you for all my many blessings, and thank you for this day that you have given me. I pray now for the safety all of us on board this flight from Atlanta to Philadelphia. I pray that you will bless the pilots and the crew and help them to make knowledgeable decisions on our flight today. I pray that you will bless this plane mechanically to ensure that all systems operate as they should function. And Lord, I pray that you would reach your hands down and wrap them around our plane and pick us up safely from Atlanta and carry us as safely and smoothly as possible to Philadelphia. I am going to place my life and trust in my hands and throw them out the window on take-off and ask that they be in your hands, and that you would have your will with my life and with the lives of my family. It is in your name that I ask your blessing upon everyone on board including myself and those that we are flying away from or home to see – Amen."

This is my prayer *EVERY* time I fly somewhere. I change the "to" and "from" cities, of course, but the rest remains the same. And if you ever happen to be sitting beside me, you will see me ball my fist, and after 15 seconds of rumbling

1

down the runway, toss my hand towards the window, placing my life and trust in His hands. (*Why 15 seconds? I do not know … I just started with that, and it has worked for over 500,000 miles so far, so not likely to change it*)

I have said that prayer for about 14 years now, since I joined the ranks of the airborne warriors, and I would say that only in recent years has it become as sincere as it needed to be. When I first started traveling, I would say it, and after the plane landed, go off in whatever city I was in to do my duty, then after work party as hard as I could until it was time to fly back home … then "Lord, I thank you …" Obviously, I was a hypocrite, but did not know it or recognize it. If when traveling we encountered bad turbulence, which seems to follow me like the plague, I would offer up more prayers *"…if you just get me on the ground and away from the lightning, I promise I will x, y, or z…"* After touching down safely, all was forgotten – back to living life for myself – chasing the dollar, no relationship with Christ, and no idea what life was really about. I believed in God, but did not have time for Him at this point in my life - unless I needed something of course.

It really became a meaningful prayer and conversation with God after the events in this book unfolded, my life to date, and I realized with such clarity what I was asking for and how I had been asking it. Before, it was simply a shout on the way out the door …*"Hey, big guy, could you take care of this for me … and I will get back to you on it later to pay my way."*

Today, I understand the magnitude of what I am asking and what He wants from me in return for delivering me

FLT # 456 ATL TO PHILADELPHIA, 10:19 AM … - PACK BAG, GET LAPTOP safely. I also realize that His will may one day be for me not to land safely, and I have come to realize that is ok as well (*although I still am not a big fan of thinking about the 'how' part*). In the words of Paul Harvey, the *Rest of the Story* will explain how I came to this place of trust and acceptance and my being ok with His will – whether that is I live to be a hundred and twenty or go tomorrow.

Chapter 2

INTERVENTION

I remember a framed copy of the Serenity Prayer on the wall of my 6th grade classroom. Someone later told me this prayer was the one shared by people who went to Alcoholics Anonymous (AA) meetings. I had no idea this organization existed or even what its purpose was. This, I was told, is the prayer shared by alcoholics in recovery. Fine by me, I suppose; I did not know any alcoholics, and I was sure I would never have to worry about AA or alcoholics. Turns out, my teacher was a card-carrying member and had been recovering from alcohol abuse for quite some time. His problem, I supposed, and as long as it did not affect me, that was no skin off my back. Little did I know how close I would get to that prayer and how real that lifestyle would become to me 18 or so years down the road.

Growing up, there was the daddy that I knew well. This was the man that taught me all those things that a good father does. He taught me that "if you're gonna be dumb, you've gotta be tough." He got me my first set of golf clubs when I was 12 years old, and we would have contests chipping to the 'plum tree' in the yard. He taught me how to hold a football and how to run pass patterns in the yard. He taught me how to dribble a basketball and to always keep my head up to see the court. He taught me how to bait a hook, how to shoot a rifle, and how to ride a motorcycle (He even let me crank the first motorcycle I ever got for Christmas in the house and ride it down the front porch steps). My daddy was an athlete himself in high school, and I did not realize it until later in life, but he so enjoyed watching me compete. He never missed a football or basketball game I played in high school, and he was on the sidelines my senior year when we won both a football and basketball state championship – I am not sure who was more proud, me or him. He was in my foursome the day I shot 68 at the Walker Course in Clemson, South Carolina, on my bachelor party weekend, and I believe his hands were shaking more than mine on every shot coming in. *(On a side note, since getting married and having children, I have never even sniffed at 68 again – something about a family and kids of your own that tend to raise your golf score, but I would not trade them for anything in the world).* My daddy would have taken a bullet for me if he had needed to, and he was my hero.

Then there was the daddy I did not know – You see, I lived in a household where I thought it was normal for the men to get together and have a few drinks, stay out late, then have the wives gripe about it for a couple of days until it died down. I had heard my mama say over and over that she thought my daddy had a drinking problem, but I thought that was just part of it … stress at work, have a drink. Keep a bottle in the truck with you in case you need a little 'snort' every now and then. Even into my college years, I always thought my mama was the bad guy, because when they fought, it was usually about alcohol – and my idea was this: If she would just leave him alone then no more fighting, simple as that. After all, my daddy was never mean to us, always provided and we never wanted for anything, it seemed. Why rock the boat, right? What we did not see was that drinking was my daddy's escape from his life – one in which he felt trapped. He had missed out on an opportunity to finish college and as such was part owner in the family logging business. Lots of history here, but let's just say that there was tremendous tension between my daddy, his brother, and their daddy – and they lived with that every day. To make it all go away, my daddy would drink - something my sister and I didn't see but our mama did. We knew he would get drunk from time to time with his buddies, and my mama would end up taking care of us – countless Christmases she would take us home and put us to bed while he stayed up to play cards or 'shoot the bull' with the boys. My sister and I just thought that was part of life - that is how it worked.

It wasn't until the summer of 1994 between my junior and senior years at Clemson University that I began to really get a feel for what was going on with my daddy. That summer, I worked with the logging operation, as I had done in the past, but this time I was old enough to pay attention. I began to notice that every day when we got home *(usually a 2 hour commute each way)* he would want to run into town to 'take care of some things'. When I would offer to go with him, he would tell me to just stay home and get cleaned up. After noticing a liquor bottle in the truck from time to time, I began marking them to see just how much drinking was going on. I soon put two and two together and realized that his running into town was his way of going off and having his drink so that I would not see him. The amounts varied, per my markings, depending on the day and how much tension existed out in the woods. One day in particular, he drank a-lot, more than one man should drink at one sitting, and he drank it in the short amount of time it took to drive to town. I could see in his eyes when he got home that he was drunk, and it all came flooding towards me – I finally knew what my mama had been dealing with for 30 + years of marriage and two emotions hit me – sorrow and anger. My heart went out to my mama for dealing with all she had for so many years, and I became angry at my daddy for doing this to himself and his family.

I was worried that his drinking was killing him – being older now, I had seen people in our town and others that had died from alcoholism. I did not want to lose my daddy. Consequently, in August of 1994 my sister, five years my senior, and I planned an intervention, although we had no idea it was called that *(this was long before the television show with the same name)*. We shared with mama what we were going to do and asked her not to be around when the intervention happened. We knew that daddy would immediately think that she had put us up to it and focus his energy towards being mad at her rather than confronting the issue of his being an alcoholic. I can recall that mama cried when we told her what we wanted to do – not tears of fear or sorrow, but tears because she was so happy that someone had finally heard her and joined her struggle – she was not facing it alone anymore. After mama left the house, we approached him – I still remember him sitting in his blue recliner, my sister sitting beside my daddy while I sat on the sofa across from him. We hem-hawed around a little and then came out and said it: "Daddy, we are worried about how much you are drinking." Actually, my sister said it as I was overcome with a dose of chicken at the time. We told him that we did not want to lose him, that drinking was going to kill him, and that if he did not stop, we were prepared to walk out of his life and not allow him to see his grandchildren (*I had no children at the time, but my sister had two*).

He told us that he did not feel he drank too much and that we were being ridiculous but that he would stop if it meant that much to us – Success! Well, sort of. Turns out, he did think that mama had put us up to it … an argument ensued, and a couple weeks later, I found beer in his truck. I confronted him with it, and he made up some story … not his, a buddy had used his truck, etc. That, my friends, is the day that I walked out – I drove back to Clemson and made do with the rest of the summer there. My sister and I invoked the do-not-talk clause on him and shut him out of our lives. In my mind I was doing it to prove a point to him, to punish him for not playing ball like we had asked him to. In my heart, I knew that I was running away from the problem because it would be much easier to deal with it by not dealing with it at all. Pride is a powerful thing, and I was allowing it to keep me from picking up the phone and trying again to help.

This estrangement went on for what seemed like forever; then slowly, we both gave in a bit and started talking to him again … I even worked with him again the next summer. But, deep down, I resented him for the way he was – he continued to drink, and he and my mama continued to argue. Fast forward a few years – I had graduated from Clemson and had a job, was married to my wife Britt, and even had our first little one, Katie Britt. We dreaded going to visit because there was always an argument, or the tension was so heavy you could cut it with a spoon (*we have sharp spoons in the South*). One thing led to another, and we fell out of graces again, my daddy and I. I was not going to be part of his killing himself with drinking; I shut that chapter on my life and did my best to stay in contact with my mama. Even though Britt and I had only moved 85 miles from them, my daddy was farther away than that from me, and I was happy. At least I thought I was. Britt calls it being an "ostrich" – sticking your head in the sand and waiting for the problem to go away. I felt guilty that I had left my mama to fight a battle that, only months before, we had told her we would join. I was embarrassed when people would ask me how my daddy was, when he was coming to see us – I would simply smile and do the same dance my mama had done for years to get around the questions. Head in sand, though, and I had it easy - I could leave and go to Greenville, SC where we now resided, and live my life without worrying about what went on back home. I did not hear the arguments nor see his drinking, so it wasn't happening. If a tree falls in the woods and no one is around, it makes no sound, right?

> IF A TREE FALLS IN THE WOODS AND NO ONE IS AROUND, DOES IT MAKE A SOUND?

10

Chapter 3

ONE IN TWENTY

"Seventeen missed calls and seven voicemails, how can that be?" That was my first thought as I got back to my car after a meeting in Tennessee. I had left my phone in the car on purpose as I did not want it to distract me while I was with a client. The location: Oak Ridge, TN. The date: April 23, 2003, a date I will never forget. I was seven hours from home and had all of these frantic voicemails from my mama, my sister, and a close friend of my daddy's. This event predated text messaging and e-mails on phones; voicemails were it … and all they said over and over were "you need to call me as soon as you can".

Before I could place an outgoing call, my phone rang again, and it was the receptionist at my company office in Greenville, South Carolina – she was patching my mama through to me. The connection was made, and my mama went on to tell me that they had rushed my daddy to the hospital, he was in the emergency room, and they were not sure that he was going to make it. They were not sure what had happened, but had pieced together this chain of events: Daddy was in the woods working when he threw up blood. He was about seven miles from a local hospital which was near the jobsite, but drove himself home

11

instead and continued to throw up blood. He tried to call mama's cell phone, but she was teaching class and did not hear it vibrating in her purse. Later, one of her students said that he heard a buzzing in her purse - her phone was ringing again; this time she answered it. It was my daddy calling her, and he said "I am at home... I need you... call the ambulance," and that was it – the line went dead.

She sped home to find him surrounded by blood and barely conscious. The paramedics arrived and rushed him to the ER – about 25 miles away (*Did I mention we grew up in a rural community?*) Upon entry into the ER, the doctors asked my daddy what happened, and he simply told them he was throwing up blood and had

been for some time. "Are you a drinker?" asked the doctor – we did not know then why he would ask such a question or what that could mean.

So, while all this was going on, I am fat, dumb, and happy in my meeting in TN. By the time they got to me, they had wheeled him into ICU, and it was there that he now lay, unconscious. But with the help of a machine, he was still breathing.

My first thought when I heard the news? *"I cannot remember the last time I spoke to him, and what if he dies without knowing I love him."* I was scared to death that I had let him down, that I may never see him alive again, and that I was too far away to make it in time. Prior to hearing those words, I had so much resentment in my heart for my daddy and could not have cared less if I ever saw him or had to deal with him again. However, in that instant, that resentment changed to fear, and I quickly realized that I only had one daddy – and I was at risk of losing him.

By the time I got to the hospital, the doctors had stabilized him – he was unconscious and drugged up from stem to stern. He was just lying there, nonresponsive, with a tube in his throat and machines beeping and blowing all around him. The diagnosis? My daddy had esophageal varices, and this is the breakdown that leads to the creation of the varices: Everything you put into your body goes through your liver to be filtered. Heavy exposure to alcohol kills the liver and causes it to not function – in the case of alcoholics, cirrhosis is the term used to describe the condition. In simple terms, it blocks the liver and prevents proper flow and filtering. As such, the blood that normally flowed through my daddy's liver began to back up … and the blood eventually began to concentrate in the veins of his esophagus. Imagine a balloon that keeps getting bigger and bigger. Eventually the skin of that balloon gets so tight and thin that it pops. In the case of the veins inside of my daddy's esophagus, they expanded to the point of bursting and spouted blood into his body – the same blood that he began to throw up. This is why the doctor had asked the first question he did when they came into the ER - "Are you a drinker?"

The prognosis? Not promising at all. I am a numbers guy, engineering major by degree, and I wanted to hear it straight. "One in twenty" was the chance they gave my daddy of making it out of the hospital … alive. That is 5% - only a 5% chance that I would ever see him alive and get to talk with him again – my daddy, my only daddy. The doctors were surprised that he had even survived the original bleeding, citing that many people bleed out before they can get help. We were devastated, and our emotions were everywhere – my mama, my sister, and I were all over the map – What do we do? What don't we do? Our emotional stability was put to a tremendous test when they called us back to the private offices after we had been in ICU for about 7 days. The doctors wanted to do a procedure to take the tube out of his throat and see if he could breathe on his own. If it failed and they had to re-intubate (*reinsert the tube into his throat*), the procedure alone could possibly kill him if the re-intubation caused the varices to start bleeding again. As the doctors and my family all sat around a small table, and with daddy's possible hemorrhaging in mind, they asked us if we wanted to sign a "DNR." I knew a lot of acronyms, but that one escaped me at that moment, and so too did the severity of what they were asking. "Do Not Resuscitate," the doctor said – "it means that if you sign this form and something goes wrong, we will let him go – It is up to the family to decide."

Are you kidding me? I am 30 years old – I am nowhere near mature enough or prepared enough to even think about that question! Well, time was of the essence, and we DID have to think about it. Your knee jerk reaction is to say do everything possible – but you soon realize that is selfish. My mama, my sister, and I decided that it was in the best interest for his quality of life that he not be made some sort of vegetable if something went wrong – so my mama signed the form, the DNR. To have to make that decision for someone's life – the magnitude of it – is incredible. It still gives me chills thinking about that meeting, that table, all those eyes watching us … I don't wish that on anyone.

Chapter 4

FRESH CUT LAWN

I did not know it or even realize it then, but looking back it is clear to see that this was one of God's pieces in my puzzle. I was so far away from any sort of relationship with Christ at this point in my life that it never occurred to me to even pray for my daddy's recovery. I had accepted Christ and been baptized at the age of 10, but I did so as I think a lot of kids do - my friends had done it, and I did not want to be left out. I don't think I was even mature enough at the time to even begin to fathom that sort of relationship. We had gone to church off and on growing up, but it never was a priority in our family. I went to church camps, then came back and did the song and dance to show off what I and the group had learned, but I can honestly say that I never felt the spirit or anything remotely close that I can recall. I even remember one lady, who will remain nameless, who told me that if I read the Bible from start to finish, I would go to heaven. Needless to say, I was not a follower of Christ back then, and somehow I made my way to where I was in life at the time of my father's hospitalization. I had a good job, a great wife, a wonderful child, and a mama and daddy who had made sure I got a college education – but I attributed that to me and my hard work – and perhaps some dumb luck here and there along the way.

So there we were, having just made a decision with respect to my daddy's final fate, and he could not even contribute to the discussion. As I said, we made the decision, and they went through with the procedure, which thankfully went off without a hitch. My daddy, although still nourished through an IV with plenty of fluids and such, was breathing on his own without the help of a tube down his throat. I remember going in by myself to him and watching him lie there with his eyes closed, helpless. I whispered to him that I was sorry I had let him down and walked out on him to fight a fight that was larger than I could have imagined. Alcoholism, as I learned through my subsequent research, is a tough foe to conquer, and I felt as if I had left him and somehow not done enough to prevent where we stood at that very moment. "I will fight with you and do whatever is within my power to make sure you make it through this – I love you, and I will not let you down again," I told him. He nodded his head as if he had heard and understood me, though he would never recall it.

Slowly, day by day, to the absolute surprise and shock of the medical staff caring for him, he began to come around and before long, he was talking with us and asking where he was and how in the world he got here. We laughed at some the things he said when he was coming off his meds – he saw feathers on golf balls as we watched a tournament on TV – he said he wanted to shave *bad ass* into his chest hair – he said he felt like we had played an Indian trick on him (*whatever that meant*) to get him into the hospital bed. Eventually, the doctors told us that he would be able to go home soon, but that his life would change forever. He would not be able to exert himself physically; he would be confined to the house much of the time; and, most importantly, if he took even one more sip of alcohol, that sip could kill him.

Talk about a fight on our hands – here is a man that had been drinking off and on for 40 or more years, and he would have to stop cold turkey – well, more like frozen turkey. We had our doubts if he would be able to do it, but we vowed to stand beside him to make sure that he was successful. We met with a counselor that recommended a program located in North Carolina that focused on sobriety. It was expensive, but we had already identified the money to make his rehab happen, although it would mean pulling nest egg funds from here and there to finance it. My sister and I both wrote daddy letters outlining our love for him and our vow to support him. The letters were strong, some would say harsh, but they were direct – if you are not going to join the fight, we cannot help you. I still have that letter saved on my laptop, and I read it from time to time – I never talked to him about it, but my mama says she watched him read the letters from my sister and me, and she could see his pride for both of us in the maturity we displayed in dealing with the situation. We were torn when he said he could win the fight on his own – without AA, without the program in North Carolina. We told him he was crazy for trying it…he was rolling the dice with his life, but we would support him doing it his way if he felt that strongly about it. "I can do it," he said. "I have to or I will die." Talk about cut and dry. Put a man's life in front of him like that, and you will be amazed at the resolve one can have.

To Do List:

CUT GRASS
GROCERY STORE
TALK TO CHRIST

The day came for him to go home, and we planned a huge homecoming. The whole family gathered at the house – daddy sat on the deck while we cut grass, cleaned the house, and just spent time together as a family – something we had not done in as long as I can remember.

The symbolism of all this didn't escape me – a fresh start, clean slate, a team formed to fight for daddy's life, and he was the team captain. We still had tons of questions about all the medical implications – would he live a year? Six months? Six weeks? – the doctors could not tell us and would not venture a guess. One senior staff member told us, "You guys have already tempted fate and beat the odds. Bobby should have never walked out of the hospital alive – there was definitely someone looking out for him to get him this far, so there is no way for us to say what is possible." *Someone looking out for him, huh?* That was the first time I thought about God during this whole ordeal. *Did He have a hand in this? If so, why would He go out of His way to save a man that had not darkened the door of a church since Moby Dick was a minnow?* That answer would come later, years later, and I had no idea at the time how clearly it would be revealed.

Nonetheless, we started off on our new journey – a new family with a new purpose and a renewed resolve. That first day home was the beginning of something that our family would come to cherish to this day and until our own days here are over.

Chapter 5

MORTON SALT

---

*God grant me the serenity to accept the things I cannot
change; courage to change the things I can; and wisdom
to know the difference. Living one day at a time;
Enjoying one moment at a time; Accepting
hardships as the pathway to peace;
Taking, as He did, this sinful world as it is,
not as I would have it; Trusting that He will make
all things right if I surrender to His Will; That I
may be reasonably happy in this life and supremely
happy with Him Forever in the next. Amen.*

Reinhold Niebuhr

I had last seen the Serenity Prayer on the wall of my 6th
grade classroom and had not given it another thought until
now. It was not until I started calling some of my daddy's
old buddies who had actually become a part of Alcoholics
Anonymous (AA) that I began to put two and two together.
I bought the Big Book, also known as the AA handbook,
and began to read it and find the answers we needed. I
gave daddy the AA handbook and several other books on

alcoholism in hopes that they would maybe spur him to get involved in the group. To say the least, his pride was in the way, and he did not want to be seen at the meetings – it was obviously tough to admit he had an issue and something that he could not beat on his own. My daddy had always been a strong man, both physically and in determination, and this was a very hard step for him. My sister and I gave him meeting schedules, called him to say we would go with him – every day, we tried to get him to go with us.

To our surprise and delight, he decided to go with my sister to a meeting in a neighboring town. She cried at the meeting, and I think she may have gotten more out of it than he did. He sat quietly, listening to the stories the recovering alcoholics shared, their openness, their honesty and, in the end, I do believe it gave him strength. That would be the last meeting he would attend – he simply had resigned himself to do it on his own, and we had to learn to respect that. He made a big step in even going to the one meeting, and we could see in his eyes that he was serious about his rehabilitation.

Our paranoia, though, was at the highest level. We called him, came to see him, checked on him – the whole time sniffing and looking for any evidence of alcohol. Roles reversed, I guess, because we were doing exactly what our mama used to do to us when we would come home from a party – we got some good laughs out of the irony of the situation, and the humor helped urge us on to keep fighting with him and for him.

Still, through it all, I never turned to God to ask for help, strength, guidance, or any answers. I was focused on letting Mark approach this just as I had all of my sporting events, college exams – whatever – I could fix this and did not need any help. At least, I was not aware that I did. I think this is typical of a lot of kids that grow up in alcoholic homes. You learn to adapt and get things done on your own so that you do not have to risk upsetting the apple cart. Stay out of the way, don't cause problems, and the arguments will pass right by – for today.

Was it the Morton Salt girl that said, "When it Rains, it Pours?" Well, regardless of whomever said it, he or she knew what they were talking about. As my daddy started going for follow-up visits with the doctors, they did the first complete physical he had had probably since playing pee-wee football *(I am not even sure they wore face masks … that is how long it had been)*. It was during this process that they noticed, after tests and biopsies of his prostate *(prostrate as my grandma calls it, but I could fill an entire book with her mispronunciations of things that would make you laugh)*, that my daddy had prostate cancer, and it had progressed quite aggressively. He probably had it for years, but when you are a man that refuses to go to the doctor, even in the sickest of circumstances, it makes it tough to get any sort of jump on maladies through early detection.

Long story short here – he underwent surgery to have his prostate removed *(cannot even say the word without thinking of my granny)*, and was set up with the program to do radiation treatments, which he completed successfully over the course of many months. No more prostate, no more prostate cancer. I share this piece of the story for two reasons: First, to further tell you how strong my daddy's resolve had gotten and how much we were being drawn together as a family without even being aware of it. Secondly, the day of my daddy's surgery, I gave him a LiveStrong bracelet *(yellow band created by Lance Armstrong*

to signify you have a story about a battle with cancer), and I put one on myself. That was November 2003, and I still have not taken mine off to this day. His? Hold that thought, and I will share that a little later.

It was God that brought him through the cancer and brought us as a family closer, right? Not in my book – As soon as my daddy was awake and I knew he was ok, I hopped a flight to Vegas to continue my plan of taking over the world.

Chapter 6

"DING"

Second chances are wonderful, especially if you are aware that you are experiencing one as it happens. My daddy's survival of both the esophageal varices and prostate cancer were both shots over the bow, but he was enjoying – we were enjoying – his new lease on life. We were a completely different family, and I saw the man that had been under that cloud for so many years but was unable to come out. For the first time in my life, as a 30 something adult, I felt like I met my father. He had disregarded the doctors' advice about staying in the house, and he kept himself busy with odds and ends here and there. He and my mama were like two teenagers – laughing together and out and about all the time – even grocery shopping *(imagine seeing your dog reading the newspaper, that is how different this was to all of us)*. They would come up for pop-in visits *(if you are a Seinfeld fan, you know about the pop-in)* and spend the weekend with us quite often. Britt and I were blessed with our second child Ben in February of 2004, and he quickly became the apple of "Poppa's" eye. Daddy loved both of our kids, and, as any good grandparent knows, let them do whatever they wanted – play with whatever, as long as they loved him, it was ok. To see them together – our kids getting to enjoy their Poppa – knowing how close we came to losing him was overwhelming, and I can say that was my first dose of perspective in this entire saga. This was further emphasized when mama and daddy went to a play to see my sister's youngest daughter perform . During the play, he told my mama, "Look at how pretty Rachel's hair is with that light glowing on it – I almost missed this, didn't I?"

Beginning in late 2003 through the middle of 2005, we enjoyed being a family. We even took a trip to Las Vegas together – hitting the strip, sightseeing, and visiting the Hoover Dam. Of all of the exciting things to do and see on the trip, perhaps the most entertaining was watching my mama and daddy experience travel and all that it implies. On the plane flight out, which was a late-nighter, most everyone on the plane was sleeping for the three-hour ride. My daddy kept hitting the flight attendant call bell by mistake, trying to turn the light on and off. Ten minutes would go by, and then he would hit it again, "*ding.*" The flight attendants were great and would simply turn it off and go back and await the next one. We got some great photos and for the first time, my sister and I had experienced a normal vacation with our parents - "*ding*".

In addition to the trips we took, some of the best times my daddy and I spent together were playing poker with some of my neighborhood buddies. We would stay up late telling stories, laughing and enjoying our time together. Daddy wore glasses that had huge dark lenses – they doubled as sunglasses and reading glasses – so he had to have them to see the cards. He became known to the group as "Ronnie Milsap" because of the glasses, and my friend even created an award for the annual poker winner called "The Milsap Award," which featured a trophy shadow box complete with a set of the glasses like daddy and Ronnie wore and cards representing a now-famous hand daddy played against one of the guys.

Needless to say, we were living the good life – everyone involved with everyone else, grandchildren excited, conversations flowing, and my daddy and I acting more like roommates than father-son. I learned a lot from him over this time period – he taught me all about the merits and pitfalls of drawing to an inside straight – I still think about him when I have the opportunity to play cards, and I can hear him saying, "There is about a one in twenty shot of catching that card, do you really think you can hit it?" Well, I do remember another one in twenty that worked out for the best. Most notably, though, he taught me about not sweating the small stuff. He had a different view of this than I did, given he was living on borrowed time – so he let a lot just roll off his back. Spots where arguments used to pop up were non-events. I was even able to bite my tongue when he took a shower upstairs at our new house in Greenville without securing the shower curtain. The water looked like Niagara Falls flowing down our light fixtures and across the ceiling … but it was ok because it created one more memory. The water marks on the ceiling, plus the hole he put in the wall with the recliner, served as his markings on our house … and again served as our reminders of putting things in perspective. It was also during this time that my daddy said something out loud to me that I knew he always had in his heart, "I love you."

At this same time, there were two parallel paths that were developing. This is where I can look back and begin to really say, *"AHA, there it was … and I did not even see it happening."* For those of you that have been wondering why this book made its way onto the Christian bookshelf in the store, here is where the story begins to take shape.

The first path to my having a relationship with Christ was paved with my daddy and his follow up visits with the doctors. He got assigned to a wonderful man whom we will call Dr. V. This man was amazed that my daddy had survived the ordeals he had and immediately focused on making sure he did all he could to keep this train rolling along. We were not aware of the severity, but the cirrhosis had caused tremendous damage to the liver, and, as a result, daddy began dying from the inside out. Slowly, but surely, his body was beginning to feel the effects of a life that had punished it. When Dr. V. began meeting with my parents, he explained to them that he was a Christian and felt prayer played a large role in people's health and recovery. As such, they would pray together at the end of all of their sessions, and Dr. V would share scripture with them. He did this not to force his agenda on someone, but rather because that was who he was. My mama told me that Dr V. was praying with them and shared how comforting it was to them. I thought to myself, *"Prayer, huh? Well, if that makes them feel better, more power to them."* I still had not tried to seek God's hand in any of this and was simply relying on the smarts of the medical staff to do all they could to fix my daddy.

Fixing, we found out, was not in the cards. *(For you non-Southerners, "fixing" means to repair as well as prepare to do something).* When the liver is damaged as severely as daddy's was, it cannot fix itself. So, other parts of the body begin to suffer, and you get some fairly strange goings on in the process. For instance, the chemicals that are normally filtered out of the body end up affecting the brain – (*Encephalopathy – for anyone wanting to Google something interesting*). In daddy's case, mama found him one night digging through the cabinets looking for a weed-eater and just talking out of his head. The cure, diuretics … you flush the body of the chemicals and voila! - back to normal. Problem is, this cycle repeats itself, and it gets more and more frequent, and the episodes are more and more severe. So, while Dr V. is navigating them through the slow degradation of daddy's body, we are pleading with him to find a cure – anything.

How do you fix a bad automobile part? You go buy a new one and replace it. With internal organs, it is the same process but a little more difficult to pull off. Go check out <u>www.unos. org</u> *(United Network for Organ Sharing),* and you can get a sense of how many people are waiting for organs – getting a new organ can be quite daunting. The other option is living donors – if you can find someone alive who is a match, the doctors can actually carve out half of the good liver from the donor, put it into the recipient, and it will regenerate itself into a full size functioning organ in a fairly short amount of time. The procedure is risky for both parties, and there are lots of things that can go wrong. Even still, I told my parents I wanted to do it – I wanted my daddy to have my liver. He had given me life, and I wanted to do the same for him.

"MARK - IF YOU'RE GONNA BE DUMB, YOU'VE GOTTA BE TOUGH" -
DADDY

My daddy refused – he said that he had gotten himself into this fix *("fix" now meaning "predicament"),* and he would face the consequences – I had a family to raise, and he would not let me risk their growing up without a daddy in order to save him. "If you're gonna be dumb, you've gotta be tough, son." We argued, we cried, and, at the same time, began to see the writing on the wall – and we are talking about life and death here, not the outcome of some football game. Daddy understood that his days were numbered and he was not going to be here much longer. We visited the transplant center in Charleston, South Carolina, and talked to the folks there about getting on the transplant waiting list. It was October of 2005 when we went, and my daddy had become a shell of a man. They evaluated him, and he was a candidate – the costs would be tremendous – the sacrifices by everyone huge, but we were prepared to do it if it could save him. In their hotel room after the visit with the specialists, daddy told mama that he did not want to fight anymore and was ready to face whatever came his way. That was it, the last hail-Mary pass we had in our bag, and it was not going to happen. I was the one that called several days later to speak with the doctors in Charleston and explained that we would not be going forward. I cried before, during, and after that call – again, I, *me*, having to be involved in those sorts of decisions – it did not seem fair, and I was mad about it, but I did not know at whom.

We asked Dr V. how much time he had … we needed to know, we had to know. His response was very honest and sincere – "live your life each day and do not focus on how much time there may be – make the most of it and love each other for the time you have left."

The second path which led me to Christ involved me and my work. Britt and I got engaged in 1995 and had set the wedding date for July 13th, 1996. The plan was made; we would both work in Thomson, Georgia, and live in Lincolnton, Georgia, where Britt's parents live. Lincolnton is adjacent to McCormick, South Carolina, where I grew up and where my parents still lived, and I had made it a point that I would NOT live where I grew up – I needed to make my own way, burn my own trails.

In late 1995, I received a letter from a software company in Greenville, South Carolina, stating it was looking for recent engineering graduates from Clemson to join its ranks – to travel the country and work with software. Britt was devastated when I told her I wanted to take the job as she did not want to move away from her hometown. It was not until later that I found out her mama had referenced the Bible (Ephesians 5:23-32) in their discussion about the move and told her living in Greenville was going to be okay. Britt told me that she wanted to move back to Lincolnton one day, and I told her it would never happen – we were our own people, and we would make our life away from the small towns that had produced us. We were meant for more, and the big city is where we would find our opportunities.

So, Britt and I move off to the big city, and I get opportunity after opportunity working for my new company. Britt is teaching school, and we are living the life and learning how to be self-supported adults one day at a time. We dabbled in churches, going here and there, visiting some two or three times, but again it was not a priority. I think Britt was looking for me to be the spiritual leader of the house, and I had no idea how to do that – so it was a standoff. Again, Christ was not someone on my "A" list of folks to be hanging out with; I could live without going to church or engaging in any time-wasting stuff like that – had golf to play, sleep to catch up on. We did this for about 9 years, until I start to get the itch to look for a new job. I had done consulting, project management, service management, product management, and had begun to dabble in some sales work – but had grown weary of riding the Wall Street wave every quarter. We were a publically traded company, and every quarter it was the same thing … revenues, profits, stock price – then start all over again. I learned a ton in the process, but I was looking for something a little different – specifically, I wanted to stay in technology, but work with a smaller, private organization. I did what millions have done and continue to do – I jumped on Monster and posted away. I was ready to ring my call button and move onto a new seat - "*ding*".

Chapter 7

FREAKS AND WEIRDOS

Recruiters are funny people. I remember the first time I ever got a call from one – I thought I must really be something if this high profile recruiter has called me, little old me, above everyone else. Little did I know that my resume was just one of probably thousands of resumes that had landed in their inbox. Furthermore, I was not aware of how the process worked – that they made money for getting you placed with a company. But as time went on, I learned the game, and I knew when someone was really looking out for me and when I was simply inbox fodder they were trying to dangle somewhere for their own good.

So when I got a call in the fall of 2004 from a recruiter telling me about another company in Greenville, I was a bit skeptical. She described the place as private, small, and focused on technology. Turns out, it was the same vein of technology that I had been involved in as of late, so my experience was spot on. The problem – she wanted to recruit me for a project management position, and I was done with that career path – I think I was good at it, but I was more interested in being in sales and working with customers on the front end. She pleaded with me to interview with the company at least once, and I told her no. "I do not want to be a project manager, so it will waste everyone's time if I have a discussion, thanks but no thanks" – we hung up the phone. A week or so went past, and she called me back to tell me that she really felt strongly that I should at least talk with these guys – about project management. I tell her in my best, defiant Mark McKinney-is-right tone, "OK, I'll do it, but I am not accepting a position as a project manager".

I get on the phone with the Director of Project Management – she asked me all the questions, and I nailed them. I was a perfect fit, and she asked me if I was interested in talking further, and I say "No, thank you. I shared with the recruiter that I was not interested in project management, but she urged me to talk with you anyway. I am sorry if I have wasted your time." She replied, "You know what, I think I should put you in touch with our VP of sales – I do not believe she is hiring right now, but you sound like someone she would like to have on her team if things change down the road."

I interviewed with Gina Magaruh, VP of Sales, and we hit it off right away. It turns out she did need someone on her team, and she liked what I could bring to the table. I met with the President, the CEO, and a ton of other members of the company – and they made me an offer. Before I accepted,

Job interview
Wednesday 10
AM call Gina on
Tuesday to confirm

I wanted to have lunch with Gina one more time with my main objective being to learn more about the people at the company. After all, if I am switching jobs and leaving my golfing and lunch buddies behind, I needed to know what my prospects were. I asked Gina, "What do people do here for fun and to unwind?" Her response: "Most everyone spends a lot of time at church and doing things with family – this is a big church-going crowd." Red Flag immediately. I can remember chewing my club sandwich and thinking, *"What in the world … do I really want to go to work somewhere that people go to church all the time … what about going out, having some beers, playing golf … ?"* I talked with Britt about it, and I can remember her response vividly, "I think it could be good. Maybe that would get us motivated to get into church more often."

I accepted the job and set my start date for March 21, 2005.

God – piece – puzzle.

My first few days on the job were typical to any new environment – getting to know everyone, finding my place, finding someone to go to lunch with and getting the scoop on everyone in the office. I needed to know who to go to for what, how to skip around the traditional political network. As I talked with some people I bonded with instantly, I soon found out that my new employer was filled with folks who had graduated or attended Bob Jones University – an extremely conservative, Christian-based college in Greenville. Further investigation led me to the true stories of husbands that would not do business travel with females in fear of dishonoring their wives; parents that had no TVs in the house due to the influence it would have on their children, and a scheduled prayer time in the conference room every Wednesday at Noon. Although I knew that I was up against some church goers when I took the job, I did not know I had stepped into this – I was surrounded by, and these are my words, "freaks and weirdos," and I did not fit in at all. I had no relationship with Christ, and if any relationship I developed with Christ had to look like what

I had seen, I did not think I wanted any of what was being sold here. However, I quickly found my own niche and did my job, head down.

Gina Magurah, the woman who had hired me, was my direct boss, and as such, she and I had the opportunity to travel together from time to time. She shared with me that she was a relatively new Christian but before had been on the fast track to success and running like mad to climb the ladder. Everyone in the office knew her story, her "event" – getting down on her knees, pleading to be saved, and an overwhelming presence coming over her – and her life was changed. On our travels, she would read the Bible and listen to Christian tapes while I played games or read Men's Fitness or something. What was most intriguing about Gina's story was that her husband Mark did not jump on the same Jesus bandwagon with her. Office talk had it that it had caused trouble in their marriage, and that they were living two different lives with this big void in the middle caused by her new found religion. That sort of made me like Mark right off. Even though I had not met him, I respected the fact that he would not be pushed into something he did not want to do. Little did I know at the time how much I would come to respect him and how much impact he would have on my life.

So as it often happens when a person is immersed into a particular environment, he becomes curious. In my case, hearing all the religion talk, I got more and more curious about this church thing. I was not into it, you see; I just wanted to see what all the fuss was about. That, and the fact that a ton of discussions at work were about "we went to church last night …and," or "the kids performed at church …," or "where do you guys go to church?" Add to it that I had gotten to be close with a few folks at the office that were actually *normal,* yet they talked about how much they enjoyed church and the time their family spent there. So yeah, I went ... what of it?

Britt and I had not found a church in the area where we could be good back-row Baptists, so we began to seek out other places we could feel at home. It so happens that our neighbors and great friends down the street attended the local Methodist Church. Folks back home, fellow Baptists, picked at us about handling snakes and such when we told them we had visited the Methodist ranks. But for the first time since we had been in the Greenville area, we felt at home, like we were where we were supposed to be. I even learned to recite the Apostle's Creed. I had one toe in and the rest of my body out of religion – it felt good to go to church with the wife and kids, then go to lunch with the "God Squad" (*that is what my buddy calls the throngs of people that hit the restaurants around 12:15 on Sunday),* but I was not all caught up in the midst of it yet – I was curious, but not convinced that I wanted to jump in headlong.

To help me along in my quest to learn more, Britt and I attended an event that Joel Osteen held at the Bi-Lo Center in Greenville. Agree or disagree with his theology, the guy can speak, and I can honestly say that he was an important stepping stone into my learning about religion. We actually saw a lot of folks from my company there, go figure. It felt good to be there, and you could feel a sense of faith all throughout the room – and it was electric.

While I am getting my orientation into the spiritual, my daddy is still fighting his battle. Dr. V continued to pray with my parents on their visits, and we all remained as positive as we could. For the first time since it all started, I was able to feel the importance of Dr. V's prayers, and I considered that there was a real possibility of getting help from above. I would later come to believe that Dr V saved my daddy's soul. My prayer life, too, began to grow and became more of a conversation with God and less of a monologue. I was learning to listen rather than just rattling off the things I needed or desired, and I can honestly say that I began to 'hear' God speaking to me for the first time – or perhaps I was just listening for the first time.

Chapter 8

A BANJO, A FIDDLE, AND A STAND-UP BASS

My mama was trying to manage my daddy's failing health all by herself while trying to continue and do her teaching job. My sister and I were doing our jobs, managing our families, and giving our mama support from afar. Daddy was rushed into the emergency room countless times as the encephalopathy episodes continued, and each time we wondered if this were the end. It was just too much for my mama to handle alone, and the next step was clear when my daddy's health continued to worsen - the white flag ... hospice. We called hospice care, and they were wonderful – a set of nurses available around the clock to help my mama and to prepare us for what lay ahead in the not so distant future. My daddy was contained to his bed at first. Then a hospital bed was brought in as daddy's health continued to race down hill; the hospital bed was easier to get into and out of. We talked with him a lot as time continued to pass and could sense the elephant in the room, but no one wanted to point it out. He was dying, and we knew it; he knew it. His pride was long since swallowed as he allowed us to help him to the bathroom and refit him with adult diapers – feeding him, bathing him, giving him his medication.

As we were handling our situation with my daddy, one of my best friends lost her daddy in a very similar set of circumstances. She described her father's last days, and it was like she had been watching us and was recounting to us the same things we were seeing. When I went to her dad's funeral, I told her I understood what her life with her father's last days had been like, and at the same time I realized that I, too, would soon be standing in the very receiving line she had just endured. I would later realize that this, too, was a piece of the puzzle and that my friends would provide me with the support I needed to get through this.

March 23rd, 2006, was a Thursday. My mama called me at work and said she thought that things were getting close and asked me if I could come and be with her – my sister was already on the way. I agreed and packed my bags. On the way to the house, I stopped by and picked up more medication – morphine to help with his pain and aid with his sleeping. When I arrived, the hospice nurses were hauling in an oxygen tank that they said would help him with his breathing as things continued to progress. I spent a lot of time with my daddy that night and the next day, and I shared many things with him that I wanted him to hear. I knew he had many concerns and loose ends he wanted to be sure were taken care of before he left us. I told him it was ok to leave us if he were ready – that I would take care of everyone and make sure his wishes were carried out. Late on Friday, March 24th, his breathing became labored while the hospice nurse on staff was there with us. She walked me outside and told me in the calmest voice, "Your daddy is passing, and you have to be strong for your family – it will not be long now, so I need you to be ready."

My sister and her family went home, and my mama, Britt, and I went inside and prepared for bed – we kissed daddy good night and told him we would see him in the morning. I woke at 7 AM and went to check on him in the back bedroom. He was cold to the touch, and I could tell immediately that he had stopped breathing – he was gone. He had left us about 6 AM, the coroner later estimated. I stood staring at the spot where he left this world – the same world he had stood and watched me come into … The irony was more than I could understand, and I cried. My mama, who had not slept a full night in probably 6 weeks, lay soundly sleeping in her bed. I tapped her on the shoulder to wake her and simply said, "Daddy went like he wanted to, in his sleep." She exploded out of the bed and was beside herself – she had lost her best friend, and there were no more good- byes, no more laughs, hugs or kisses. Britt called hospice and told them that he had gone, and they began the process that had been planned well in advance. I called my sister and said, "It's time", and she knew. We held on the phone silently, not sure of what to say, even though we knew this day would be coming. How can you be prepared for something like this? … You can't.

The next few hours were frantic with friends and family coming in, the coroner, the stretcher being wheeled out, the funeral director, the plans, the tears, the embraces. It was over and yet it had just begun. Daddy was cremated *(his final wish)* the following day and before they began, the funeral home supervisor called me. "Mark, your dad has on this yellow Livestrong bracelet – what should we do with it?" "Leave it on," I told him, "We promised each other we would never take them off ." And we have not.

My daddy was a huge fan of bluegrass music, and our family wanted to honor that at his funeral. We decided to make it a celebration of his life, and I began a fevered search for someone to play bluegrass music at the service. Seems an easy task given we were in the heart of some of the greatest bluegrass musicians in the world – but it was not. I did, however, manage to find a friend of a friend of a friend in Greenwood, SC. He had a band, a bluegrass band, and he agreed to do the service. I told him what we wanted to play, and he assured us he would take care of it. The service was led by my mama and daddy's preacher from days gone by, an 85 year old man who touched us all with his message. Two close friends shared stories, and we laughed and cried at the same time. The music was perfect – banjo, fiddle and stand-up bass supported the singing of *Amazing Grace, I'll Fly Away,* and as we departed, *Old Homeplace.* I know daddy was tapping his foot and smiling at what we had pulled off.

PLAYLIST: AMAZING GRACE, I'LL FLY AWAY, OLD HOMEPLACE

As anyone who has lost a family member knows, we were busy over the next weeks and months with death certificates, letters, insurance and supporting each other. I leaned on my friends that had recently lost their dads – four of them, all my age, who were already members of the 'dead daddy club' that I had now joined. I also leaned on God, although I was not sure how it was supposed to be done. I prayed for Him to take care of my daddy and to wrap his hands around our family. My faith was somewhat strung together, but growing, and I vowed to make it stronger because in the moment I lost my daddy, I realized that I wanted to see him again and there was only one way that could happen.

Chapter 9

TWO PAIR: OVERALLS AND MARKS

> *"It is better to take refuge in the LORD*
> *than to trust in man.*
> *It is better to take refuge in the LORD*
> *than to trust in princes."*

Psalm 118: 8-9

I began to pray every day ... *"Lord, if you feel the timing is right and I am ready ... please come into my heart and help me to understand how to live my life so that I can be with daddy again"* ... nothing, no lights, no big bang ... nothing. I began searching the Bible for answers, but it was like Greek to me. Britt and I threw ourselves more heavily than ever into church so that we could find more answers. I varied my prayer, thinking that I was just *asking* the wrong way: *"Lord, help me to live for you so that I can see my daddy again – save me from myself and my sin. Give me strength to know you and to support my family."* Interestingly enough, Britt knew nothing about what was going on inside me – I was embarrassed to tell her what I was up to, so I bottled it up.

And then, I went straight to the source himself, my daddy. If he could hear me, he would not let me down. So I spoke to him one night as I lay down to go to sleep. *"Daddy, if you are up there and this whole thing is for real … show me. Give me some sort of sign that you made it and that I am not looking for something that is not there. If it is not real, I don't want to waste my time trying to get to see you again."* That same night I woke up and saw a glow at the end of the bed. I rubbed my eyes to try and wake myself … but I was still sleep drunk. As my eyes cleared, I could see my daddy standing there at the end of our bed right beside the ironing board *(that I had forgotten to put up the morning before)*. He was wearing his favorite set of overalls and an old tee shirt. I said "Hey, buddy, what's up?" and he nodded at me without a sound. I tried to continue and focus, to make him clearer, but the vision was still so blurry, and he faded in and out. In an instant, he was gone, and I lay there trying to figure out if I were nuts, dreaming, or if I had really been given the sign that I had asked for. Could it be that simple? I woke Britt up and told her I had just seen daddy. She told me that she believed me and was sure that he was there with us. I am sure she fell back to sleep thinking I was a lunatic.

As I woke the next morning, I had forgotten the whole thing. I was in my closet getting dressed when I pulled a shirt and its hanger off of the top row and I dropped it. It did not fall all of the way to the floor, however. The hook of the hanger had gotten caught in a loop of something tucked back behind the hanging clothes – it was my daddy's overalls that had been folded neatly and placed in the back of the closet when we had come from his house the last time – and the night before came flooding back to me. I sat down and held the overalls in my hand … wondering, hoping and trying to make it make sense. *Was this just some cruel coincidence? God – piece – puzzle?*

That was in April, 2006, a few weeks since daddy had gone. I held onto that night as I continued my search for answers, but as time passed, I convinced myself that it was just coincidence and some weird twist of fate that had made me drop the shirt and have it hit his overalls. So I was back to looking for an even more clear answer, but I had still not felt God's hand on me or had an overwhelming shudder – I had no Gina moment, so obviously God was not listening or either I was just not worthy of being on his team. Or even still, maybe the whole thing *was* just a crock as so many people say about religion.

Fast forward to June 9th, 2006. Mark Robert Magaruh, Gina's husband, was killed in a motorcycle accident. His services were planned for June 13th, 2006, and all of the office went to support Gina. I attended as well, with no expectations. I was going to a funeral, just like I had so many times before, and I was there to show my support – nothing else.

Mark Minnick presided over the service at Mount Calvary Baptist Church in Greenville, SC (http://www. mountcalvarybaptist.org), and he shared openly about how Gina had come to know the Lord and how strongly Mark had fought it. This entire service is available for download at www.FaithonaStickyNote.com and I encourage you to listen to it – it will change your life - it changed mine. He shared how Gina's faith had come to be through a discussion she had with a co-worker years before. Gina had asked her co-worker Sam what he thought would happen if he died that day – right that instant. Sam's response, "I am saved, so I am going to heaven." No wavering, no what ifs, no conditions, he was confident. Gina was not, and it bothered her to no end. So she started her search which culminated in her salvation the night she got on her knees and asked the Lord into her life. This came as a shock to Mark who had gone to sleep with one person and woke up to find another in her place. So years go by, and they are living their lives together but separate. They had moved to Greenville from Chicago, and Gina had become involved with Pastor Minnick's ministry. Before long, Mark sought out the Pastor to get some answers. Minnick explained that if their marriage were going to survive, Mark needed to learn more about this religion stuff Gina was so in love with. Bible studies started, and Mark slowly began to learn more and more about life and about salvation. He asked Pastor Minnick one day in an effort to gain clarification, "So, you mean if I go out today and have a wreck on my motorcycle and die without being saved, that I am going to hell ... to hell?" Pastor Minnick advised him what the scripture sets forth, and Mark sat back in his chair and let it soak in.

Their studies continued, and Mark slowly began a walk with Christ, although still not saved. He confided with the pastor that he had been praying to be saved but that it had not happened ... no event, no big bang. This is when I sat up in the pew ... *this guy was just like me. Go on ... tell me more.* Well, Mark continued to pray, and it did happen – he felt his life change, and he was happy to report that he had been saved, but on "my own terms" as he shared with the pastor. He went on to say that the world was a hard place, especially for someone declaring to be a Christian, and before he put himself out there he wanted to be sure he would walk the walk. Pastor Minnick went on to share that at 11:33 AM EST, the day of his death, Mark sent an email to Gina with a piece of scripture: Psalm 118: 8-9, which reads as follows:

> *8 "It is better to take refuge in the LORD than to trust in man. 9 It is better to take refuge in the LORD than to trust in princes."*

GRIP 2x4 WITH BOTH HANDS, SWING LIKE BASEBALL BAT, AIM DIRECTLY AT CHEST, FOLLOW THROUGH

I was overwhelmed and felt like I was the only one in the room, and that pastor Minnick was speaking directly to me. He went on to share the message of the service through Luke 16: 19-31, which is the story of The Rich Man and Lazarus.

Luke 16:19-31
(New International Version)
www.biblegateway.com

The Rich Man and Lazarus

19 There was a rich man who was dressed in purple and fine linen and lived in luxury every day. 20 At his gate was laid a beggar named Lazarus, covered with sores 21and longing to eat what fell from the rich man's table. Even the dogs came and licked his sores. 22 The time came when the beggar died and the angels carried him to Abraham's side. The rich man also died and was buried. 23 In hell, where he was in torment, he looked up and saw Abraham far away, with Lazarus by his side. 24 So he called to him, "Father

Abraham, have pity on me and send Lazarus to dip the tip of his finger in water and cool my tongue, because I am in agony in this fire." 25 But Abraham replied, "Son, remember that in your lifetime you received your good things, while Lazarus received bad things, but now he is comforted here and you are in agony. 26 And besides all this, between us and you a great chasm has been fixed, so that those who want to go from here to you cannot, nor can anyone cross over from there to us." 27 He answered, "Then I beg you, father, send Lazarus to my father's house, 28 for I have five brothers. Let him warn them, so that they will not also come to this place of torment." 29 Abraham replied,"'They have Moses and the Prophets; let them listen to them." 30"'No, father Abraham," he said, 'but if someone from the dead goes to them, they will repent." 31 He said to him, "If they do not listen to Moses and the Prophets, they will not be convinced even if someone rises from the dead. "

It was as if someone had hit me in the chest with a two-by-four *(which has happened before, so I know the feeling of which I speak)*. I immediately went back to the night I had asked my daddy to reveal himself – *was he my Lazarus, was he coming to my house to tell me, to warn me?* Why was I sitting here in this very spot today given all the choices I could have made in my life? I had turned down job offers from other companies, yet I was here – I had met Gina, and I was now listening to her husband's funeral service. So many that day struggled with why Mark had been taken, but it seemed so clear to me that he had been taken so that this message, this very real message, could reach someone in the crowd - and I was convinced that it was me. Pastor Minnick closed the service by asking us to all bow our heads and for anyone that wanted to receive Christ in their heart to simply raise their hand above their head so that only he could see. I slid my hand up and heard him say, "There, I see you, God bless you".

God-piece-puzzle.

Chapter 10

ANYONE CARE FOR "PI"?

"There are only two ways to live your life. One is as though nothing is a miracle. The other is as though everything is a miracle."

Albert Einstein

So by now, I am getting a pretty eerie sense that there is something more to life than 9 to 5, paychecks, and taxes. The circumstances seemed too strange to be anything else given all the different paths that I could have taken in life, but I was here – right here.

So with the recent events of Mark's funeral on my mind, I continued my quest to learn more and more. We continued to go to church with our friends and were blessed to be in the presence of so many believers, both at work and in our regular lives. We still lived, though, our normal lives. We had not turned into some kind of Bible-thumping yahoos running up and down the road. The reason - I *still* convinced myself that there had to be a clearer answer – I mentioned that I hold an engineering degree, and I needed to see it in black and white. Pi = 22/7, 3.14, right? I needed to see

Pi before I would really get it. I figured that if God were real, he was probably putting his hands on his head and screaming to the top of his lungs "What more do you want me to show you?"

As does happen, time marches on and the day that we knew would come, a day that we had dreaded, did indeed arrive - the anniversary of my daddy's death. Britt and I were in Greenville, but we had all planned - my sister, her family and us - to meet at mama's house to be together. We were not sure what we were going to do; we just figured we were *supposed* to be together ... that is what people do, right? Well, given that we were going to eat lunch at mama's house, Britt and I decided to catch the early service *(one of the best things created since sliced bread)* at the Methodist church which would give us time for church before the ninety minute drive to McCormick. We had never been before, but we had to take advantage of it on this day, Sunday March 25th, 2007 - 365 days since my daddy had passed away. So we walked in the church and took a bulletin, a little sleepy, but still ready to hear a positive word before we went to face the sadness of the day. The early service is a little more contemporary – youthful, high-energy music, which we looked forward to. As the musicians prepared to play, the leader of the group addressed us: "Good morning, everyone, and welcome to Simpsonville United Methodist Church. We are glad you here today, and we know you came to worship the Lord. We are going to do something we have never done and spice up our music a little this morning by adding in a banjo to give it bluegrass flair. If you turn to your bulletin, you will see that we are going to start with *I'll Fly Away*, please sing along with us…" How could that be? How could they play that with a banjo today ... today of all days? Another two-by-four right across the ribs!

I could not look at Britt, and she could not look at me. I felt like my legs were going to leave me, and the entire room began to spin. I held on tightly to the pew, trying to keep my faculties as the banjo was picked and the congregation sang "...one fine morning when this life is over, I'll Fly Away ..." This was it, this was Gideon's fleece (Judges 6: 14-16, 36-40), and it was covered in dew, just like I had asked.

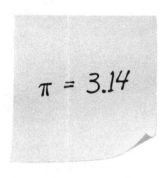

It all came flooding back in an instant ... the job interview, the people I thought were freaks and weirdos, my working with daddy, 5% chance to live, DNR, Dr V, three years of time together that we did not deserve, overalls, Mark Magaruh, Luke 16: 19-31, Lazarus, Mark Minnick, Vegas, poker, banjo and bluegrass ... "I'll Fly Away" on the anniversary of his death ... my daddy was telling me that this is for real, and Pi = 22/7.

We drove to mama's house, and I went in to give her a hug. I handed her my bulletin, still clutched in my hands, and showed her the first song – "Can you believe it?" She didn't say a word, but she did not have to. I knew that she could sense it, too.

Chapter 11

GEORGIA ON MY MIND

"*It is not the critic who counts: not the man who points out how the strong man stumbles or where the doer of deeds could have done better. The credit belongs to the man who is actually in the arena, whose face is marred by dust and sweat and blood, who strives valiantly, who errs and comes up short again and again, because there is no effort without error or shortcoming, but who knows the great enthusiasms, the great devotions, who spends himself for a worthy cause; who, at the best, knows, in the end, the triumph of high achievement, and who, at the worst, if he fails, at least he fails while daring greatly, so that his place shall never be with those cold and timid souls who knew neither victory nor defeat.*"

Theodore Roosevelt
April 23, 1910

Men are strange beings, and I can say that with conviction because "*I are one.*" We have ways of saying things and doing things that only we can understand, and we tend to get frustrated if someone asks us to explain or justify what is obviously a great decision. After the bluegrass episode and all else that led up to it, we visited my mama and Britt's parents a lot more – and one Sunday afternoon, just like a light had gone off, it hit me – I want to move my family back home (*McCormick, South Carolina, or Lincolnton, Georgia*). For about 11 years the thought would almost make me nauseated when Britt would bring it up, and I had been so dead set against it. However, on that Sunday afternoon riding through the area, it was as if it were written in the clouds. I told Britt, "I want to move to Lincolnton." I have only rendered her speechless a few times in our long history together, and this goes down on record as one of those. She was elated but wanted to know why – why now? Why, so suddenly, had I changed my mind when I was so dead set against it? Imagine someone growing up hating Mayonnaise, and then one day for lunch asking for a Turkey sandwich LOADED with the stuff – same sort of deal here.

I did not know why at the moment or even understand what the implications would be for my job, but I was sure of one thing: I wanted to move to Lincolnton, Georgia. For once in my life, I had made a decision and decided to let all the cards fall where they may with respect to everything else – *Don't sweat the small stuff. Right, Daddy?* Although in this case, a job, a house, a family – all things like that hardly qualify as small stuff . Nevertheless, we started looking for property to buy so we could build, and we also checked out existing homes we could buy, somewhere to lay our heads. I spoke with my boss about making the move – he did not want to tell the executives right away as we were going through an acquisition (*"we" being acquired by "they"*), and he was not sure how the new management would react. This went on for some time, and we slowly watched the housing market begin to make its decline. Supply began to overwhelm demand to the point that I finally just had to do it – we were moving, and I was going to put our house on the market. Sign made, FSBO - we were official.

We found a house in Lincolnton that was perfect and that meant we would not have to build; thus, we avoided the death of one of us, Britt or myself. I truly believe that if we tried to build a house together we would either drive each other insane or to our ultimate demise, whichever came first. It took us eight months to sell our house in Greenville, which meant months of the lovely double mortgage. Paying for two houses, two taxes, two insurances – felt like Noah and the Ark with so many twosies, twosies. We struggled along, and as people do, we found ways to make it work. Towards the end of our house selling, I prayed: *"God, if you will please just bring the right person in front of us, we will deal with them and negotiate to come to an agreement – just give me the chance to negotiate – but do it in Your timing."* Two days later, an offer came in on the house – a way low-ball offer, but it was what I had asked for, right? The opportunity. So we dealt, and we dickered … and we sold our house. I have never told anyone that I prayed that prayer, not even Britt, and many would say that it was simple coincidence, but I know in my heart it was not. It is difficult to describe, but when the call came in from our realtor, it was as if I just knew God was saying, *"Ok big boy, here is the opportunity you asked for, now show me what you are going to do with it."*

Things worked out at my job – as long as I had access to an airport and could get from A to B, I could live on Jupiter. Lincolnton was closer than Jupiter, so all was well. Britt ended up getting a teaching job in the very high school she graduated from back in 19 … well, I will leave that to her to disclose. We settled into our new home and began to get reacquainted with some old friends. We were where we were supposed to be, I felt, but was not sure why we were here. Why was I supposed to be in Lincolnton – I had showed up, now what was I supposed to do? We took advantage of some of the things we had learned in Greenville, and I began to look for properties we could buy to begin building an asset base. I joined two partners, and we bought an old run-down gas station in middle of town and turned it into a restaurant. Another partner and I have since opened up a fitness center in the town - a service that was previously not provided and one that we think is greatly needed. And I wondered, *"Is this what I am supposed to do with my life – is this why I was brought to Lincolnton, so I could be part of building up value-added services in the area?"*

At about the same time, I equipped myself with the readings of *Rick Warren and Purpose Driven Life*, and it hit me that perhaps it was not what I could do for Lincolnton that I should be looking for, but what Lincolnton was supposed to do for me ... what was I supposed to experience here that would grow me?

Britt and I became involved in the church immediately – going every Sunday. I also got into Sunday school, which is something I had not been to since I was a young boy. I went because one of the teachers was and still is a good friend of mine who had turned his life around about 10 years back when he said he felt the Lord calling him out. I remember the night he told us; we were riding in the car on the way out to eat ... Britt and I so far away from anything Christ would have us do, and Lee Bo told us that the Lord wanted him to change his life, and he was going to follow whatever He directed. *"What a fruit loop",* I thought under my breath – *"Where is the Lee Bo I know and who is this goof ball sitting in my car?"* But somehow it was different now. Although I still did not understand what he meant by being called, I could at least respect his position and become part of his Sunday school class (*he actually team taught with the preacher, two Sundays a month*). So there I sat, in worship service and Sunday school every Sunday … but I still had not had a moment like my co-worker Gina experienced, even though I had continued to pray about it. Without fail, our preacher would touch on it every Sunday – some story about someone being saved and feeling a healing hand, hearing angels, whatever …me, still nothing.

WILL THIS SERVICE
EEEEEEVVVEER
EEENNNNND????

To add to the frustration of the nothing I felt, our worship services began to run long every Sunday … EVERY Sunday. I mean in the 12:30 range, 12:20 … just long. All of my black buddies laugh at me and say that is early for their services … but suffering from my self-diagnosed A.D.D. (*Britt says A.D.H.D.*), it killed me. I would get out of church and be fuming … *why did I have to sit there and listen to this for that long?* And it wasn't just me; it was the majority of the congregation. I got so mad that I decided I had to talk to the preacher, Dan – something had to give, and I felt like if no one else was going to talk to him *(funny how people think it is blasphemous to disagree with the preacher),* then I was. So I did it – I set a meeting and went in and talked with him, and it was great. I explained that we had a group of young people *(young to me … 30 somethings, ok?)* that had thoughts and opinions on things we could do in the church to grow it. We all got together and shared our feelings, our ideas for how we could get more people involved, etc – one of the main ideas to come out of the discussion was, go figure, an early and more contemporary service. Dan said he would consider it and talk it over with the deacons, but that it would require work on our end and our commitment to growing it. I will admit that the main thing I was looking to get out of this was just that – out! Out earlier on Sunday so I could be free to do whatever – I had no problem putting in my time, as long at that time had a specific start and end. *God-piece-puzzle.*

Turns out, the deacons agreed and gave their go-ahead to try it. Only one problem left to address. As I mentioned before, Dan team taught with Lee Bo for the Sunday school class – two Sundays a month. If he were going to do an early service and the regular service, he needed someone to take the Sunday school class in his stead. He emailed me the following note *"I will need you or someone you enlist to teach Sunday school in my place. No way I can handle three in a row! (Don't ask someone without talking to me about it, but I do think you would be a good facilitator/leader for the class)."*

I immediately began to think of who could I get to teach this class so that the master plan could take effect. One more brick in the wall, and I would have it sealed up – early church, then Sunday school, and a free man by 11 AM. And the full magnitude of his note started working on me … *Was he asking me to do it? Did he really think I should do it? Did he really think I **could** do it?* I showed Britt the email, and deep down I had hoped she would tell me that I should just do it … that was the push I needed. If she said it, then it would not be my decision – I would just be doing what she thought was right. But she did not tell me I should do it. She said that another man would be great at it, and we should recommend him for it. So I emailed Dan back and told him Britt's pick, and that was that. He agreed with the choice, and we paged down on that item.

Three or perhaps four days went by, and this thing was killing me. *Why did I not tell him I would teach the class?* – This urge I felt was so strong. This was where I needed to be, and this is what I needed to do. For whatever reason, I was supposed to have said yes to him when he asked me, and I was supposed to be teaching that class. I told Britt first, and she said, "...Well, yeah, I think you would be good at it, and I think it would be good for you." Geez, why did she not just say that in the beginning? I mustered up the courage and emailed Dan - "I want that job, let me do it." You could sense that this was what he was looking for all along, and he gladly accepted my offer, but said he wanted to talk with me first. *Car caught, now what do I do with it?*

Chapter 12

THE COACH

"I would rather live my life as if there is a God and die to find out there isn't, than live my life as if there isn't and die to find out there is."

Albert Camus

I went in and met with Dan and talked over the new job of Sunday school teacher. Believing in full disclosure, I told him that I needed to get a few things out in the open lest he be surprised one day when he saw me rolling out of the local grocery store. You see, I do drink a beer on occasion – watching football games, grilling, on the boat at the lake – just casual. I, of all people, know the power alcohol can have on the body, and I respect that. However, I needed him to know that if he saw me coming out of the grocery store with beer in the buggy, I did not want to feel like I had to run and hide. In other words, I told him, I did not want to feel like I had to lead two lives – one in the pew and the other in plain view. If I were going to take over teaching the class, I had to do it as Mark McKinney, the man God had placed in this very spot at this very moment. I think that is the trouble a lot of people have with religion in general – they think that once you become part of the church, you have to stop being you. No more letting curse words slip when you hit your thumb with a hammer, no more admiring an attractive person walking down the street, no more enjoying a glass of wine at dinner. God knows every move you make and every thought you have, and if you are not going to hide it from him, what good does it do to hide it from your preacher or even the old lady down the street for that matter? You know when you are committing a sin, as does God – and the beauty of having him in your heart is that you begin to notice when you are straying and you *want* to learn from your mistakes and not repeat the same behavior again. The important thing is to live a life that makes God proud so He can say: "Well done, good and faithful servant." In short, you begin to change from the inside out which soon begins to show itself from the outside in – into others eyes and hearts.

"Just don't let what you do hurt your witness," Dan told me as we agreed that I could teach the class– "that is most important." My first response to him was that "I ain't going to be a witness to others," thinking that he meant standing at the airport with a sign or banging on doors. His response: "Mark, as a Christian, you <u>cannot not</u> witness." In other words, people are watching you and whether they see the good or the bad, they see your witness. Very similar to my job as a sales rep today – all of my customers are references to others. They are either positive or negative, but they are references nonetheless. *(The well known fact in sales is that negative references tell 10 people while positive references tell 1 – can you see a similarity with Christians?).*

I will have to admit that this struck me at my very core and made me realize that I did have to be aware of my actions in front of others. I could be myself, but that self had to be aware of the team I was supporting. I then asked Dan how I would know if my witness was genuine – how would I know if I was leading my life as He would desire? Dan then gave me these nuggets which serve as a very clear measuring stick to answer that very question:

- Your actions show if your faith is real.
- If there is no change in your life, then you do not truly have Jesus in your heart.
- If your life is not a reflection of your relationship with Jesus, then you have no relationship with Jesus.
- If your "have to" for God changes to "want to" for God (i.e, I have to go to church becomes I want to go to church).

"MARK - DON'T LET IT HURT YOUR WITNESS" - DAN

That talk with Dan would not hit me full force until weeks later, but it did, and it became even more evident that to enter into a relationship with Christ meant that your life did change and you are held responsible every moment of every day for your decisions – not just for how they would affect you, but for how they may affect others. Out of that talk, I also recognized that it was OK to have my own opinions about church and about religion, and, most importantly, it was ok not to have all of the answers because being a Christian is a life-long learning experience. Previously, I felt like if I questioned anything at all about the subject, it would show people that I did not believe in God, and that I was indeed a have-not. I was never more ready to do anything before me than to embrace the

Sunday school class – not just for what I could teach others, but for what I could learn in return.

My Sunday was coming up – it was the Monday before, and I had a whole week to prepare what I was going to say. Tuesday, I had almost a whole week to look at the lesson – after all, they gave you a teacher's guide to go by. Wednesday, couple of days wasted, but still time. Thursday and Friday – who can think of planning for something all the way on Sunday – it is the weekend. Saturday – that was lake time, we had all night to prepare something. Saturday night came, and I found myself reading through the lesson for the week trying to make it make sense to me … what did I need to teach the people, this group of my peers who would be waiting with bated breath to see how well or poorly I did. Then it struck me – I have to tell them how I ended up in this room – I had to tell them why I sit in the seat I sit today. I threw the lesson book aside and focused on putting together all the details of my life that had led me to this spot – the same details that you have read so far – my life, my testimony. It came slowly at first, then began to pour out of me and onto the back of a sales proposal that I was writing it on. I went to sleep, not telling Britt what I was planning - because if I did, I would have to do it, and if I told no one, I could call an audible at the very end. All during the early service, I continued to update my notes, careful to cover the page so that no one could see what I was writing – my heart began to slowly creep into my throat, which is odd for me. I would rather speak in front of people than anything else I can think of, even if I have nothing specific to talk on – I am just a ham.

So then came the time, 10 AM, D-Day was upon me, and the room filled with people – more than I had ever seen in there before. Coach Larry Campbell, legendary football coach of our beloved Lincoln County High School football team, was there as well - Georgia's winningest coach in high school football and ranked 2nd in the nation amongst active coaches *(as of this writing)* for wins. Turns out, Coach, as we call him, had normally gone to the older men's class *(no offense, Coach)* but had not been in quite some time. He had decided to hang around since the early service had just ended and asked the preacher where he should go – and my class was it; there he sat. No added pressure or anything from a man that had seen many star athletes perform under pressure – I hoped I was one of them.

"The Seat in Which I Sit," I told them, was the theme of the lesson today. I explained that I would not be teaching Sunday school but more so leading the discussions – I was not a Bible Scholar, nor did I think I would ever be, but I did have some curiosities and hoped I could bring some flavor to the discussions. I told the group that before they accepted me as their Sunday school leader, I wanted to tell them how I got to where I was, the seat in which I sat. And then I started, I rattled off my entire testimony – first time ever. I remember thinking months before this day, just thinking one day, I don't have a testimony, and here I was giving one. We laughed, we cried, and during the process, I had an epiphany that I shared with the group. "I always felt broken because I never had my moment ... my Gina moment. But I realized something in the process of putting my testimony together – I have had many moments." As I stood there in front of that group, it again came back to me so clearly – my daddy's life had been spared so that I could find my faith; I had ended up with my new job so that I would find church and have the strength to deal with my daddy's death; I met Gina and was at Mark's funeral so that I would hear his story and the message of Luke 16: 19-31; I was led to Lincolnton, Georgia, so that I could sit in the pew and get mad enough to go see the preacher, and I had been challenged with the teaching job so that I could stand there that day and realize how it all fit together – how my

daddy's death had saved my life, and how it was my purpose in life to share his story with others so that they and I may enjoy a stronger relationship with Christ.

About three weeks later, I had the opportunity to talk with Coach in a quiet room as we were waiting for Sunday school to begin, and he told me something that changed my life and is one of the primary reasons you hold this book in your hands right now. "Mark," he said, "I have no idea why I ended up in your Sunday school class a few weeks ago because I usually just go home. But for some reason, I felt like I needed to stay that day, and I asked Dan (preacher) where I should go. I was embarrassed when he told me to go in with the younger folks, but he assured me it would be ok. I want to let you know that I have been to a lot of preachings/teachings and revivals, etc., and your testimony touched me so deeply in a way I have never been touched before. My relationship with Jesus Christ is stronger today than it has ever been as a result of being there that day, and I just feel like I needed to tell you that."

Coach went on to tell me that one of his biggest fears is speaking in front of people, although he gets asked to speak a ton based on his notoriety in the game of football. He said he normally turns down every one that comes along, but one came up a week earlier, and he had decided to give it a try. He addressed the crowd and told them that he was nervous, and that he had prayed for strength to get through it without stumbling, and he asked them to pray for him as well – and they did; he could see them. He started his message off like this – "I normally do not do these things because I do not like public speaking, but let me tell you about something I experienced a couple of weeks ago. A young man who I know only a little stood in a room full of people, some of which he barely knew, and gave the most honest, revealing testimony I have ever heard. So I decided to myself that if he can have the courage to do that, maybe I should have the courage to do this …," and Coach did. *God-piece-puzzle.*

And then it made sense to me – what I had been looking for all along – the reason I am here, the reason anyone is anywhere – it is to have an impact on those around you. As a Christian, it is to live your life in such a way that causes others to look at themselves and want to ensure they are living for Christ. Through my relationships, experiences, and study, I have tried to find something that would keep me focused on the absolutes every day – those things that would keep my eyes on the prize, my salvation. The following are what I firmly believe are the keys to a successful Christian walk. At least I hope that I am right, because that is how I am attempting to live mine. In short, this is my faith on a Sticky note, how I strive to live my life everyday as an outward expression of my Bible reading, internal study, and quiet time. As a recommendation for your quiet time, find something to do every day to keep His word in front of you – there are thousands of daily devotionals that you can buy or to be had for free at your local church.

BE DISTINCTIVELY DIFFERENT; BE AN ALIEN

IT IS OK TO LOVE THE RELATIONSHIP AND HATE RELIGION

BE AWARE OF YOUR WAVES

WHERE DID YOU SEE GOD?

DON'T MISS IT

Be distinctively different; Be an Alien

I heard Mr. Paul Reviere preach a message on this very subject one Sunday night *(which is another strange thing as I hardly ever make it to Sunday evening service, but I was there to hear this)*, and it has stuck with me. His point of the message was simple – we live in a world that makes it tough to be a Christian with so many influences to take you in another direction. In order to live the Christian lifestyle, you have to live counter-culturally–as an alien amongst the masses. You get the picture, right? If some little green man were to walk into the grocery store, everyone would notice immediately that something was different – that this little fellow was indeed an alien. The same should be true of our Christian walk – we should live our lives so that people say, "There is something different about that person, and I want know why." We have to get our own lives in order before we can begin to truly show others Christ is in our hearts. Similar to the flight attendant instructions you will hear before every flight you take: "The cabin is pressurized for your comfort and safety. In the unlikely event of a cabin depressurization, oxygen masks will appear overhead. Reach up and pull the mask closest to you, fully extending the plastic tubing. Place the mask over your nose and mouth, and slip the elastic strap over your head. Tighten by pulling on the ends. The bag does not need to inflate for oxygen to be flowing. If you are seated next to a small child or someone needing assistance, secure your own mask before helping others." The first time I heard this, it was counterintuitive to me, but as I have begun to understand more about the Christian faith and my responsibilities, I know that is certainly accurate. Before I am able to offer help to anyone else and be of service, I have to first be able to show that I walk the walk before I talk the talk. Remember Mark Magaruh?

Set your life as an example to be followed by others by doing the things the Bible teaches us in its simplest terms – kindness, forgiveness, love, compassion, giving. Be distinctively different than the world around you, and you can have tremendous impacts on not just yourself, but those people you touch. Put God first, then others, then yourself in everything you do, and see how rewarding your life can be. It is difficult, believe me, and I struggle with this one daily.

Being an alien can involve doing some of the simplest things you can imagine. For instance, Britt and I will often go into a restaurant and without them knowing it, pick up someone's check and pay for it. Easy, not expensive, but a small token that will then carry over into that person's life and perhaps influence *them* to do something nice for someone else. Cracker Barrel is one of my favorite spots to eat when I travel, and I will often ask a waitress to slip me someone's check but without letting that person know it. You see, if you tell someone you are doing it for them, you end up doing it for *you* and not for *them*. Another simple way we practice being an alien is by giving a larger than normal tip to someone – especially someone that appears to be having a bad day. Instead of a $2 tip on a $10 meal, try leaving them $20 one time and then slip out of the door. If your heart does not feel rewarded, check your pulse.

It is ok to *Love* the *Relationship* and hate *Religion*

In a subsequent message preached by Mr. Reviere that I had the good fortune to hear, he shared this little nugget that again has stuck with me: If we get all tied up in the Xs and Os of religion, it tends to mire us down. Should I be Baptist, Methodist? ... Should I be dunked or sprinkled? Should I clap in church or sit quietly? Is it okay to go to church if I don't have on a tie? … whatever. Hearing this message, I realized that I do hate <u>Religion</u> and in large part think that it is what kept me for so long from having the <u>Relationship</u> that I needed. Live your life with Christ in your heart and enjoy knowing that He is always there with you – whether you be on top of the mountain or under a heap of rubble at the bottom. Knowing that the tests you face in life are just that – tests, and each with a lesson to be learned on the other side.

By the way, growing up, I had always heard that the biggest difference between the Methodists and Baptists is that the Methodists would speak to you at the liquor store. Focus on your relationship, and let the religion go by the wayside. Your life will be better for it.

Be aware of your waves

In the summer of 2009, Britt and I were crazy, stupid, or fortunate enough to buy our first boat. My friends had always told me that the two happiest days of a man's life are (1) the day he buys a boat and (2) the day he sells the same. Nevertheless, we did take the plunge since we do live only a stone's throw from the water, and we got ourselves a pontoon. One of the ways we use it to spend time as a family is to pack a cooler with food and drink, head out in the evenings to find a quiet cove, throw out the anchor, and fire up the grill. One particular evening we had done just that and had just begun to cook the chicken and asparagus that Britt had prepared. We heard a boat coming down the lake at a pretty good speed and could see off in the distance that the driver of it was passing us by. He went out of sight, and we could barely hear the engine of the boat anymore, but we soon began to get the effects of his passing. The waves rolled into our boat, and we began to rock back and forth and up and down. The grill tipped a bit, and the grease fell onto the burners causing flames to shoot up – Britt yelled at me to put it out - I yelled at her to leave me alone – we both yelled at the kids to get out of the way. After all the dust had settled, Britt looked at me and said, "You know, the guy in that boat is long gone, and here we are fighting as a result of his waves, and he has no idea." A little later, another boat passed by, this time while our kids were swimming alongside our pontoon. They laughed and splashed as the waves lifted them up and tossed them back down – they loved it.

And then it hit me clear as a bell – that is the same way our lives are. We go along everyday, and we cause waves with our actions, some good (*for swimming*) and some bad (*grill fires*), but what we do affects others in ways that we will sometimes never know, just like the guy in the passing boat. If we live our lives according to God's will, we have the opportunity to affect others in ways that we may never be aware, but that can have eternal impacts on them and perhaps the people around them.

So everyday, I remind myself that what I do, how I react, and the image I project is a wave that will at some point crash into someone else. I do my best to make all of my waves good ones, and I am convinced that this is one of the most powerful ways that I can minister to others and have them see Christ in my life.

Where did you see God?

We started this in our Sunday school class, and it has been quite a powerful outlet for people sharing how God has impacted them throughout the week since we last met. The concept is simple – where did you see God this week? Make note of it and embrace when you see God working in your life. It may be the birth of a child. It may be your stopping just in time before you ran into the back of a car in front of you. It may be a sunset or a rainstorm – but take note. My challenge to you is to look for God every day and then share it with someone. It will begin to change your life and that of the person with whom you are sharing. Write down your encounters with God, and at the end of the week when you think your life is in shambles or that you have had a bad day, pull the list out and read it.

Don't Miss It

Mr. Hillyer Wright, a man that I have grown to know and respect, taught me this. He first presented the statement to our Sunday school class and asked what it meant to us – what does it mean not to miss *it* – what is *it*? Our discussion ensued, and it was clear that as Christians we should not miss the opportunity to influence someone's life for Christ, to tell how our life has changed as a result of our relationship, to help someone cope when they may be facing a struggle they think they cannot overcome. As well, if you are a lost soul who has not yet been saved, you should not miss the opportunity when it is presented. It may in the form of someone asking you to lunch, to church, or a ballgame, but the point is this: *Don't Miss It!* I took this to heart because for so long I thought that in order to influence someone's life was to go knock on doors and hand out Bibles or to corner some guy on a plane and ask him if he had heard the "Good News." Not so much. Our responsibility is to take advantage of those opportunities that are put before us and NOT MISS IT when it happens. We may see those opportunities every day, or they may only come along once in a blue moon – but when they do, don't miss them. Our lives will be defined by the dash on our tombstones, so make the best of every opportunity while you are still in yours. Mark McKinney 1973 " – " 20xx. Make the most of your dash.

I have been fortunate enough to attend the Masters golf tournament since I was a child, most of my first ones with my daddy. Then and now, you can go to the front gates and see a gathering of people with signs waving and some men talking loudly about how we are all going to hell if we don't repent – how our lives are full of sin, and we should come and talk to them about how we can be saved. The scariest part to me is that they have little children holding up signs as well … some of them not old enough to read or have any concept of what they are waving. Without fail, that turns me off, and I do not respond to that sort of display – maybe some people do, and they have come to Christ that way, but not for me. I have learned much more and been influenced far more deeply through a quiet conversation with someone about how Christ has impacted his life or the lives of those around him.

Chapter 13

RED CORVETTES

"For whosoever shall be ashamed of me and of my words, of him shall the Son of man be ashamed, when he shall come in his own glory, and in his Father's, and of the holy angels." - Luke 9:26

I remember being in a class at Clemson and discussing the power of the mind, persuasion, and suggestion. As an exercise, the professor asked us this simple question: "When was the last time you saw a red corvette?" I had no clue the last time I had seen one, and at the time, I could not remember if I had ever seen a red corvette in my life, knowing deep down that I had. "Class dismissed, have a great weekend." If my memory serves me correctly, I believe it was 7 red corvettes that I saw before returning to class on Monday. Had this professor pulled together some grand scheme to ship in tons of red corvettes to Clemson, South Carolina, so that his class would notice them? "No," he assured us. "They were there all along."

As I began my Christian walk in the heart versus just on a head level, one of the first things I was concerned with was people labeling me a freak and a weirdo *(talk about turning the tables, huh?).* I felt like I was stepping out into Yankee stadium naked and just waiting for people to begin their chatter. But as it turns out, that did not happen at all. What did happen was that I began to see red corvettes. I began to notice that all around me were firmly grounded Christians that I had never even seen before – coworkers, friends-both old and new, and family. I noticed that Tim Tebow, University of Florida quarterback and Heisman winner, wore Phil 4:13 written in his eye black during games. Britt is the cheerleader sponsor at our high school, and I was floored at all of the girls that are out in the open with their faith. What a blessing! I was shocked and surprised at how many status updates on Facebook I began to notice for the first time – perhaps a verse for the day, perhaps a prayer request, or simply a "Thank you, God" for something or another – but I noticed them, and I realized that this was a pretty cool club to be a part of.

There are fellow Christians that I work with now, and I am so blessed to have known them and been impacted by them. We can talk now, about faith, about our respective walks, and we can lean on each other for support when maybe no one else will understand. I smile now when we go out to dinner while on the road together and pause before attacking our salads – to bow our heads and say grace for what we are about to receive. What an eye opening experience when you begin to share your faith with others – to find out that you are not the only one who struggles, and that is okay. That is what God expects of us – to try and to fail, then to get up and try again.

If you have not picked up on it already, I am somewhat of a golf fan – probably nursed by those first trips to Augusta, Georgia, with my daddy when I was a kid. It is interesting that this sport as well would present me with red corvettes of its own. April 8th, 2007, Zach Johnson held off Tiger Woods to become the winner of the Masters tournament. He could have said anything – about how proud he was of himself, about what the money would mean to him and his family – but he said this: "This being Easter, I cannot help but believe my Lord and Savior, Jesus Christ was walking with me. I owe this to him." Zach does not know me from Adam, but hearing him say that touched my heart. While I continued to struggle a little bit with "being out there" with my faith, here is a guy that stood in front of millions and shared his. April 18th, 2009 - Britt and I were with friends at the Heritage Golf tournament on Hilton Head Island, South Carolina. Lee Janzen strolled down the 16th fairway, and I could see written on his hat: John 14:6. I am by no means a memorizer of scripture so was embarrassed to say that I did not know what that verse was specifically. We got back to the condo of a friend's grandmother, and I found a Bible and began to search for the verse. "What are you looking for?" one of the young ladies in the room asked. "Just a Bible verse I saw on a hat, John 14:6: *I am the way and the truth and the life. No one comes to the Father except through me,*" she said. And with that, 10 or so young adults standing adjacent to the Harbour Town golf links talked about scripture over a table of cheese balls and cocktail wieners. Lee and Zach were not ashamed of their faith, and that meant a lot to me. In addition, they had opportunity, and they did not '*Miss it*' – they made good waves, and I hoped I could do the same.

What I quickly came to realize is that being a Christian does not mean you have to paint your house a different color, sell all your stuff, and fly to Uganda to be a missionary. It does not mean that you isolate yourself from the rest of the world and live within your own four walls. It does mean that you have accepted the responsibility to live your life according to His will and as a reflection of your relationship with Him – it's that simple.

I am still a "learning Christian" and know that I do not do everything right. Britt and I still argue, we still fuss at our children, and we still struggle with stress, issues at work, and trying to keep up with schedules that don't always seem doable. One of my biggest struggles is at our annual sales meetings where I have always been one of *the guys* – always ready to hit the town, stay out late, and whoop it up with the best of them. It may seem small, but it is a challenge to tell all of the people that expect you to be the life of the party that you are heading in to watch the late news – I am realizing now that this is an opportunity that I should not miss. But, at the end of the day, Britt and I have established a Christian home in which to raise our children and are becoming more open with sharing our faith. I am still not comfortable being asked to pray out loud, and I even dodge the blessing at our family meals from time to time by asking one of the kids to say "God is Great ..." or "Lord come down and be our guest..." It is okay, though, not to have all the answers and to question things within your faith – that is growth and that is learning. You don't have to be perfect ... just be in the game. I do not have all of the books of the

Bible memorized, and I could not win a sword drill against my boxer bulldog, but I am in the game, and my life is better as a result. In our Sunday school class, I don't try to teach everyone who migrated from where, who was oppressed by whom, etc. I facilitate discussions based on the teachings of the Bible amongst people who share a common bond in Christ so that we can grow, learn, and cope together. The question we base our classes on is this: If you were convicted of being a Christian, would the prosecution have enough evidence to convict you? Well, would they?

Gina had asked her friend Sam what would happen to him if he died that very day, and he knew that because of his relationship with Jesus Christ, that he would reside in Heaven. I am blessed to say that I can now answer that question with confidence as well and that '*some glad morning when this life is o'er, I'll fly away.*'

If you are not yet saved, but desire to have that relationship with Christ, simply pray the following prayer and then go and share with a pastor that you have done so – your life will never be the same.

> *Dear Lord,*
> *I admit that I am a sinner. I have done many things that don't please you. I have lived my life for myself. I am sorry, and I repent. I ask you to forgive me. I come to you now and ask you to take control of my life; I give it to you. Help me to live every day in a way that pleases you.*
> *Amen*

Traveling a lot, I have the opportunity of seeing and being seen by a lot of people – in airports, restaurants, planes, hotels, etc. People often ask me about my Livestrong bracelet: "Why do you wear that thing on your wrist?" And

I just smile and say – "Let me tell you a story about my daddy."

God – piece – puzzle.
"Ding"

Acknowledgements

A lot of experiences involving many people went into defining my life as it is to date and as a result, the stories that make up this book. I wish to thank everyone at every turn that had an influence on my life, and I would like to extend a special thanks to the individuals listed below for the very personal and very special impact they have had on me and their help in making this book a reality.

Larry Campbell – "Coach" as we call him had a great deal to do with me sitting down and putting pen to paper and creating this book. I knew him only as a legend when I first met him and now I am honored to call him a friend and a brother in Christ. Coach has shared a great deal of perspective with me and shown me that it is ok to be open with your faith as well as to have questions as you continue to grow.

Bridgette Cliatt – a very close friend and someone that I am very thankful agreed to be one of the first reviewers of this project. Bridgette offered great perspective and candid feedback on the first drafts, and I thank her for her time and insights.

Tim Collins – although not mentioned by name in the book, Tim stood by my daddy's side after he got out of the hospital and gave him the friendship he needed at a time that could have been very bleak. Words cannot express how much I appreciate the support he gave daddy.

Lisa McKinney Crawford – My older sister (she loves it when I say that). We have a common bond through the loss of our father which I know has made us both stronger. We still pick on each other today and have a twisted wit and love to make each other laugh.

Gina Magaruh – First my boss and now my colleague and true friend. Gina can only be described as a 'rock' and her courage in the face of tragedy and her dedication to her faith serve as an inspiration to me.

Betty C McKinney – My mama and the lady who made me what I am today. I thank her for everything she has done for me in my life and for the opportunity to experience the events of this book alongside her. We are closer today than we have ever been, and I look forward to her teaching my own children the things she impressed upon me as I grew.

Britt Mattison McKinney – people always told me I 'married up', and I certainly believe that to be true. Britt is an incredible woman and I am proud to call her my wife, the mother of our children, and my best friend. I thank her for her patience with me and her continued support of me as I continue to grow in my faith.

Mark Minnick - What a huge piece in my spiritual puzzle Pastor Minnick was – I am so grateful that I had the opportunity to meet with him and to continue a relationship and fellowship with him today.

Lee Bo Partridge – great friend, strong man of faith, and one of the funniest folks you will ever meet. Lee Bo jumped into the pool first, and although I thought him crazy at the time, he showed me and others that it is ok to live a life of faith.

Paul Reviere – straight shooting and unashamed man of God. He is my neighbor, my friend and has been a great influence in my life.

Dan Rosser – a man I am delighted to call my preacher and my friend. Without his work in my life, I am not certain that I would have ever come to the spot where I am now in my faith – and I thank him for that.

Craig Smith – a coworker, friend, and fellow Christian who was kind enough to agree to be one of the early reviewers of this project. His insights and feedback were very helpful, and I thank him for his assistance.

Randy Smith – the man that I tricked into being the editor of this book. I asked Randy to 'help me review some of the text to make sure it flows' and before you knew it, he was head down editing the entire thing. I thank Randy for his time, his effort, and his patience with me through the process.

Dr V – A God send for our family and a true 'good guy' in my book. He provided our family support medically, spiritually and emotionally and we will never forget the impact he had on my daddy.

Hillyer Wright – salt of the earth man and someone I am thankful I have the privilege of knowing.

Afterword:

A LOT HAPPENED SINCE 2010

They say that what some see as a bad circumstance could really be a blessing in disguise, and I had to take that to heart when the 2010 publisher of this book shared with me via letter in 2015 that they were shutting their doors. My first reaction was to do nothing, which I did, and did quite well for a long time. However, the more I thought about the original reason I had written this book, which was to share my testimony and perhaps have an impact on bringing someone to Christ or encouraging someone to strengthen an existing relationship, I realized that I needed to stop doing nothing and find a way to keep on keeping on.

That you are holding this in your hands right now is evidence that I did in fact find a new publisher in 2017, and that *Faith on a Sticky Note* remains a living and breathing entity.

In addition, out of bad circumstances many times comes opportunity, and this is no different. Since the original publishing of the book, a lot has transpired that I have often wanted to find a way to "get in" the book, and by virtue of going through a re-publishing, if you will, I got that chance. This additional chapter represents a summation of the things that have transpired S.T.O.P. (since the original publishing), and I am proud to have the opportunity to share them with you here.

For starters, as soon as the book hit the street, the response I received from friends, family and complete strangers that I came across was absolutely humbling. Sharing your faith can be a scary limb to step out on, and I was so pleased that doing so had afforded me such an opportunity to connect or reconnect with so many people who were touched by what I had shared. I had many people tell me that they, too, had questioned their faith and thanked me for saying it "out loud." I had the opportunity to speak at several churches to share my testimony and speak to the stories in the book in more detail. I even got to speak at the church where I had first gotten baptized when I was 12, and what a great perspective it gave me to realize how far (and wide) my path back had been.

There were two particularly interesting opportunities that came about that would have never have happened had I not stepped out on that limb, and I want to share them here.

First, I had the opportunity to create a new friendship through an interesting set of circumstances that included a flight to the West Coast, on which I sat beside someone who was very close to Coach Dabo Swinney from Clemson University. Long story short, I had read Dabo's testimony, and it was not unlike mine in that it involved a family life impacted by alcohol. I sent him a copy of my book through the person I had sat beside on that flight and never thought any more about it. Fast forward a bit, and by another strange set of circumstances, Coach Larry Campbell (remember him from chapter 12?) was at Clemson for a football camp and ended up talking with Dabo, and for some reason mentioned that Mark McKinney was his Sunday school teacher. Dabo said, "I think I have a book by that guy in my bathroom." Later that same day, while I was driving in my car, my cell rang with a number I did not recognize, and when I answered I heard "Mark, this is Coach Swinney up here in Clemson … Coach Campbell and I were just talking about you, and I wanted to let you know that I enjoyed your book, and I appreciate you sharing your faith."

We talked for about 10 minutes and eventually ended up meeting, and I am thankful to get to call him a friend to this day. His strength of faith has been an inspiration to my entire family (and we are partial to his results on the field as well!).

Second, after I published my book, my mom had shared that she was reading a book called *When God Winks* by a gentleman named SQuire Rushnell, which looks at these events the author terms Godwinks. These are, by his definition, "An event or personal experience, often identified as coincidence, so astonishing that it could only have come from divine origin."

For those unfamiliar with Mr. Rushnell, he is a former ABC network executive who led Good Morning America to the top, and is a father of Schoolhouse Rock (sing it together now … conjunction junction …). After leaving television, Mr. Rushnell decided to pursue inspirational speaking and writing, which, of course, led to *When God Winks*.

I began reading my mom's copy and realized that my entire testimony—the things I had originally thought coincidences—were actually Godwinks, and I simply had to reach out and tell Mr. Rushnell. I sent an email to him thinking that I would never hear back, but was surprised when one of the first entries into my website guestbook was from him offering words of encouragement. He and I ended up setting up time to talk via telephone and spent close to an hour talking about faith, Godwinks and life in general, and here I sat and marveled at the fact that by simply sharing my faith, God had opened up this door to connect two people who would have otherwise never crossed paths in a million years. Mr. Rushnell and his wife, Louise, have written some very powerful books and offer great resources for growing closer together through prayer that I encourage you to research and utilize in your own life.

In addition to the amazing doors that were opened, the new relationships I was able to form, and the old ones I was able to strengthen, I knew there was something that I absolutely had to do. Remember I shared that when I got baptized I did it to impress a girl? Well, I knew I needed to make that right, and I did. After the release of the book in 2010, I rededicated my life through baptism for all the right reasons and the most important part of that to me is that my kids were able to watch me do it. Since then, they have both been baptized, for all the right reasons as well, and that has made me more proud than anything else they could ever accomplish.

Proverbs 27:17 teaches us that "iron sharpens iron, and one person sharpens another" and one thing that is clear is that if you are to continue to grow in your faith, you absolutely need to find some iron. I found mine through, again, a strange set of circumstances (surely you remember me *just* talking about Godwinks) whereby I met someone on a business trip and through a conversation he shared something that has become such an important part of my life. He suggested I take a look at getting involved with F3 (f3nation.com) which is a men's workout group with the mission to plant, grow and serve small workout groups for the invigoration of male community leadership. The three Fs are Fitness, Fellowship and Faith and truly, in my estimation, represent men living out Proverbs 27:17, and I have been blessed beyond belief by the iron I have found therein. I would encourage you to check out the website, find a location that works for you, and give it a try. Tell them that F3_Nomad sent you!

As a final update, I share something that I never really paid a lot of attention to in the first publishing. Someone very close to me who is an active participant in Alcoholics Anonymous shared after reading the book, "This could really do a lot to help someone battling addiction."

I said, "What now?"

I had been so focused on the faith side of the writing, that I had no idea that the story itself could have the potential to help someone overcome a battle with addiction in their own life—that my dad dying of addiction could serve as a big red warning light to someone that this is not a fairy tale and you do end up facing the consequences for bad decisions. Couple that conversation with another I had shortly after that with a friend and former colleague that I had not seen or spoken to in years since we worked together at the same software company. Clay Cutts had seen a Facebook post about my book, had read it, and reached out to me to share that although most people never knew it, he had battled addiction for much of his adult life—even as he and I had worked together. I never knew and had never at all suspected, and he and I were able to reconnect around the topic and talk through how our paths had diverged and had now come back together.

It turns out Clay had become a certified addiction counselor and was now on a mission to help those that needed it. Through that work, Clay was writing a book to serve as a resource for people struggling with addiction, and I was humbled that he asked me to write his foreword.

And it is in sharing that foreword below that I give you the last update on what has transpired in my life since the original writing. It is proof that God continues to work in our lives every day, and that, through his power, we have the opportunity to impact change not just for today or tomorrow, but for hundreds of years to come.

Beyond the Bottle
Author: Clay Cutts
Foreword by Mark McKinney

July 12, 2013 is the day that I took my last drink of alcohol. Prior to that, May 4, 2013 was the last day that I had anything to drink at all—beers with the guys while we played golf. I remember that May day very clearly—golfing, playing cards and having one more beer, then another, and I said to myself, "I am 40 years old and tired of this; I don't *want* another beer!"

It all washed over me in an instant, like a wave that finally catches a kid running out of the ocean. The wave crashed, I stood up and collected myself, and was convinced that I just did not want to drink anything anymore. So what happened in July? My wife and I celebrated our 17th wedding anniversary, and we had a bottle of wine with dinner. I woke up the next morning and felt like a failure because I had let *myself* down by not sticking with my vow not to drink again. I had not done anything dumb that night—no fights or arguments, no hangover—but the pain I felt was worse because I had failed myself. Why was it such a big deal? Let me give you some background.

My story may be a little different than most. You see, I am not an alcoholic, but based on my family history, I have every opportunity to be. My father died in 2006 at the very young age of 62 from cirrhosis of the liver. He was in fact, an alcoholic in a family tree that had many such branches, and had been drinking for as long as I could remember—not the come-home-drunk, knock-the-door-in, slap-everybody-around drinking, but the drink-with-the-guys, have-a-drink-to-escape-work, occasionally-embarrassing-at-parties, arguments-with-the-wife kind of drinker. In my eyes, he was the normal husband/father doing what I thought every man did. Initially, I was sad that he was gone, but then I became angry that he was missing seeing my kids grow up, and more so, they were growing up without their granddaddy!

Even so, I did not let that stop me from continuing my lifestyle of social drinking (which, as many of the readers will attest to, began at an early age by sneaking beers out of my dad's cooler), having beers with the guys, being that guy at a party from time to time, and then I was struck by something I read in a book in early 2013. *Every Man's Marriage* was given to me by a friend, and one piece of the book talks about the importance of *your* impact on your family tree—that the decisions you make today will affect every generation to come whether it be five years, 20 years, 50 years … 100 years or more down the road. The writer offers this: "At some point, every man must decide: Will I purify my branch of the tree, or will I allow this poison to seep through the generations, leaving the job for a better man down the line?…"

As I said earlier, the wave finally hit once I let it catch up to me, and this is what I finally realized: most of the dumb decisions I have ever made involved alcohol, 90% of all arguments with my wife were a result of drinking and not being in control of my emotions, 99.99% of all stupid situations I ever found myself in were a result of alcohol, and if I did not do something to stop the cycle **today**, then I was not just risking *my* life, but I was putting my kids, their kids, and their kids' kids at risk. I could not fathom seeing my children battle alcoholism one day and know that I had steered them there. I had to be the one to purify my branch, so I did, and I have. My son, who was eight at the time, said to me one day, "Daddy, I noticed that you haven't had any alcohol to drink in a long time and I want you to know I am proud of you!" Now that is changing a family tree!

I met Clay Cutts in the late 90s while we were working together at a software company in Greenville, SC. I remember thinking he was one of the smartest people I had ever met; he could solve any problem thrown at him, and I was glad he was my friend! Clay had an amazing approach to problems (it was the dot.com era, so we faced a ton), and I loved to watch him work. Our paths diverged, though, and we went our separate ways, losing touch as many former workmates do. It wasn't until 2010 that our paths would cross again, in a way I never imagined.

Following the events of my dad's death, I had written and published a book that focused on his addiction, his death, and its effect on my life. Through the wonders of social media, I got a note from Clay one day that said something to the effect of, "Mark, I never knew about the struggles with your dad ... and you probably never knew that I, too, am an alcoholic."

We reconnected, talked at length, and shared our stories with each other, and I could tell then that Clay had a gift for helping others in similar circumstances. I remember saying to him, "If you could have spoken to my dad 10 years ago, he would be alive today!" And I am so proud and excited to see that with *Beyond the Bottle* Clay is doing just that; he's helping dads and mothers, husbands and wives, daughters and sons—you and me! Clay did not know it until later, but the conversations he and I had about addiction planted the seeds that prepared me for my wave in May of

2013. Through this book, Clay offers such practical advice and guidance from the perspective of someone who has fought and continues to fight the same battle. He is an incredible player-coach, and I know he can make a difference!

I encourage you to approach this book not as a book—don't just read it and log it away in your mind. Approach it for what it is—a lifesaver for you, or for someone you love—and put in the effort to change your life today. It is not by accident that you are holding this book in your hands right now, and one day you may look back and realize how significant this moment is. And recognize that the changes you make today aren't just for you; you hold in your hands the power to change your family tree forever, and that's a mighty long time.

God bless and my prayers to you for your strength.

ORDER INFORMATION

To order additional copies of this book, please visit
www.redemption-press.com.
Also available on Amazon.com and BarnesandNoble.com
Or by calling toll free 1-844-2REDEEM.

CPSIA information can be obtained
at www.ICGtesting.com
Printed in the USA
FSHW020411110720
71627FS